This small book is an important contribution to Holocaust memoirs. It is an extraordinary story of survival and one that should be shared in schools and preserved in libraries. Students will be inspired by Stan's struggle for survival and unfailing courage.

—Jennifer Smith

Teacher, Sacred Hearts Academy Honolulu

A Boy in Hiding is a very real, up close and personal view of what it felt like to live in Holland during the German Occupation. Reading this book which is written through the eyes of a child will give you an idea what courage really is. You will not want to put it down.

—Wally Amos

Author, *Be positive, Blue Mountain Arts*

This book is a must read for school students all across the country and would be a great addition to any school library. Rubens' story of his childhood flight from Nazis, shows how a boy's courage and resilience can overcome even the most horrifying circumstances.

—Beverly Creamer

Reporter, *The Honolulu Advertiser*

A BOY IN HIDING

Surviving the Nazis
Amsterdam
1940-1945

STAN RUBENS
WITH
RONNY RUBENS

Zea Books: Lincoln, Nebraska, 2016

Second edition.

Designed by Kira Fulks http://kiraproductions.com/

ISBN 978-1-60962-089-9 paperback
ISBN 978-1-60962-090-5 ebook

Zea Books are published by the University of Nebraska–Lincoln Libraries.
Electronic (pdf) edition available online at http://digitalcommons.unl.edu
Print edition available from http://www.lulu.com/spotlight/unllib

Dedication

To my daughter Ronny Rubens Garcia
and my grandson Grayson Garcia
In memory of the many family members who lost their lives

Acknowledgments

*With deep gratitude
to my daughter Ronny,
my publisher Jim Riordan, designer Kira Fulks
and to The Sidney Stern Memorial Trust
for bringing my book to life*

Contents

Introduction

Stan Rubens

Honolulu, Hawaii—2005

Before reading this book, perhaps it will help to set the stage, so to speak.

Amsterdam is the capital of the Netherlands. The city of The Hague is the seat of government. However, Amsterdam is the largest city in the Netherlands. Because Holland is such a small country, it is often overlooked. It borders Germany to the east. Belgium is south of the Netherlands. On the west is the North Sea and if you took a boat sailing west, you would get to the coast of England (see map included in Family Album).

The Netherlands has so many names it's almost confusing. We are called the Dutch. The language we speak is Dutch. We live in the Netherlands, which is often called Holland. Or the French refer to it as "Les Pays Bas." Literal translation: "The low lands," a correct statement since at least 40 percent of the Netherlands is below sea level.

The Dutch have mastered redeeming land from the sea or lakes. Their formula is simple: Build a dike around the lake you want to redeem and follow up by pumping the water out of the "diked" area.

Simple, but still it takes technology, refined over the years and already in practice at the time of the Second World War. This means that about half of Holland (or the Netherlands) is crisscrossed by dikes that surround low land, anywhere from three feet or more lower than the dike. Those lowlands are called polders.

These days, with good highways going from Amsterdam to the German border, travel would take you about two hours. Of course, in the old days, going by foot would take perhaps a good week or so.

It was easy for the German Army to invade the Netherlands. They virtually ran over the Dutch Army. They flattened the city of Rotterdam by bombing it with their Luftwaffe (airforce). The Dutch Government surrendered shortly thereafter to the German occupation and the Nazi Regime. Only 20 percent of the Jewish population survived the war; 80 percent were killed, mostly in the gas chambers of Dachau and Auschwitz.

This book is written from the point of view of an eight-year-old boy growing up too fast during the following five years of the war. Therefore, there are no lengthy diatribes describing different seasons, or conjecture of different possibilities, or lengthy character descriptions. Those are not the way an eight year old sees life, especially under the pressure of the Nazi regime.

I view the relationship with my father different as a grown man than when I was a young boy. It must have been very grueling for my father to help his family survive under incredible and difficult circumstances.

It wasn't until my late twenties that I fully understood my father. It does not change what happened. It took time to understand why my father was the person he was.

A number of his eccentricities were lifesavers. His

need to be important and to show off by carrying a large bankroll in his hip pocket, kept the family money out of the hands of the Nazis. His bravado was often embarrassing. Now I know that it saved our lives.

My mother's role seemed totally passive, as all decisions were made by my father. Actually, my mother lacked the experience and insight to deal with our survival, that notwithstanding, she came up with ideas that kept us going. She was a silent force, not to be underestimated.

I have been able to reconcile myself with the way things developed. And the way my father behaved. I often believe that there was just no other choice. During the war, I was mostly left to myself and, therefore, had to fend for myself. I spent very little time with my parents. I still do not know if this was good, bad, or indifferent. Somehow it must have formed me as the person I am today.

During the war and later in life, I realized that so many people were willing to help me or do things for me without asking for anything in return. I am still deeply grateful, as many put their lives in mortal danger for me. Now I often try to do things for others, even if they are total strangers.

Many locations described in this book are no longer there. The Westeinde Street address where we were sold out to the Nazis is now a major banking structure. The countryside where American pilots dropped food into the polders is now residential homes. I did not recognize anything on one of my trips visiting the Netherlands some time ago.

To say to you, dear reader, enjoy the narrative: Well, that would be a misnomer. One does not enjoy stories of the war, knowing the outcome was the death of a conservative estimate of 6 million Jewish lives and 5-6 million Christian lives. Victims of the Holocaust included those people considered a threat to the Nazi's, or those that might have been instrumental in helping Jewish people. Also, Homosexuals, Gypsies, or any person against or unwilling to accept the Nazi yoke. Nonetheless, there are moments of enjoyable memories. I can think back with merriment on some of the events that remain vivid in my mind. And I come to an understanding and an acceptance of the zest of life—the good and the bad, experienced in so many multifaceted ways.

Prologue

Ronny Rubens
Los Angeles, California—February 2005

When I was a child, I thought that being underground meant that my father was literally hidden underground like some pesky gopher crawling his way through the dirt. I imagined that he hid under layers of strata, cautious and sensitive to the movements of the earth above him. Always nervous that some large grisly hand would reach down through a hole and drag him out by the hair on his head. My father's childhood stories were captivating. With my father as the sole actor and me as the sole audience member, I became fascinated with his world. Transported to the places of his childhood, I became the secret companion that he didn't have. The child who hid with him.

With his descriptions, I supplied a sound track in my head. The bombs going off. The unknown voice of my grandfather, Jacques. The fearsome sound of boots on the cobblestones. With his narrative, I became the cinematographer and inserted the background: the tall anemic apartment buildings of Amsterdam. The glassy tops of the canals. The perpetual gray of the sky.

Over time, my father's stories have become my own. These are stories that I have slowly told other people. His history is mine as well.

In my father's stories of war, I imagined him desperate, lonely, and always drastically skinny. Tense and alert for the SS soldier that would come to take him to the gas chamber like so many before him. I pictured how my father, desperate for food, would steal from the bread truck. How he would have to walk with his head down, afraid to make eye contact. Afraid that he would look at someone and they would give him away. After all, he could not hide the way he looked. Dad talks about how he used to cover the Star of David sewn on his jacket with another sweater thrown nonchalantly over his shoulder.

He doesn't realize that he still does this today. Subconsciously hiding a star that isn't there.

I grew up wondering who in my circle of friends would become the SS soldier and who would become my father. A victim. A child of war.

My father once told me this story: On the momentous day that the war had ended he ran outside and ran through the meadow that was near the house. The sunlight was so bright that he had to close his eyes and run blindly for a few minutes before he could open them and see what was left of his country. His home.

At one point, he heard something and instinct told him to lay low. Don't breathe, someone might hear. But then he looked up in the sky and saw what he had heard. There, in the sky, like Pegasus coming to save him, like the ultimate hero at the end of a movie, my father saw American bombers flying over him. They dropped something from their low-slung wombs and my father ran over to see what it was.

SUPPLIES!

Bread and food and medical supplies. For the people that had gone hungry for a long, long time. Dad looked up and waved to the low-flying American Liberator in the sky. He wondered if they could see him. Smiling, he took a bite of the very white bread. It tasted like cake. Bread that was sacred to the people who braved the war. Bread he would crave for years to come. A craving I inherited. America must be a wonderful place, he thought. Someday I will go there. The war was over and he was once again free to be a child. Free, period.

"Dat," he told me, "vas da day da bread fell from da sky."

I'll never forget that story.

There came, towards the end of this writing, an urgency from my father to finish the book. To be done with it. Why, only he can express, but I presume there is a need to excavate the memories as quickly and sensibly as possible. To simply, let it all go. Many holocaust survivors have found solace in telling their stories. A purging that, once finished, leaves them exhausted but finally relaxed, like a terrific sneeze.

My father, and others like him, no matter what they are or what they became, are still children of war. They have spent a lifetime with their memories. Dad is anxious to finally share his, not only in the hope that people will understand, but that he will, too.

Family Album

Remaining photographs

My paternal Grandmother

She dies in Auschwitz Concentration Camp

A rare family photograph, circa 1944:

From left to right: my sister Ronny holding yarn; Chris the boarder; Little Beppie with her fist raised; Jos in overalls; Gerard is just visible behind yours truly, the author at age 13. Seated, is Aunt Beppie; foreground hunched down, my buddy and Nemesis at the same time, Johan.

7

Right:

My mother and sister— circa 1932

Left:

My mother just after the war

The Author:

   Age 14— just after the war

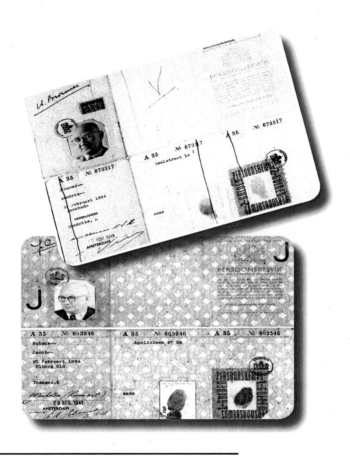

I.D. issued by the German Occupation to my father

Note the "J" stamped in the corners, denoting a person is Jewish. Fingerprints shown are included for positive identification.

Passport issued to my father after the war
The indetifying "J" has been eliminated

Rare Photos:

Top:

    Window display at my father's retail store—circa 1938

Bottom:

    A renovated display of my father's store—after the war

The Author:
  Left—age 15
  Right—age 19

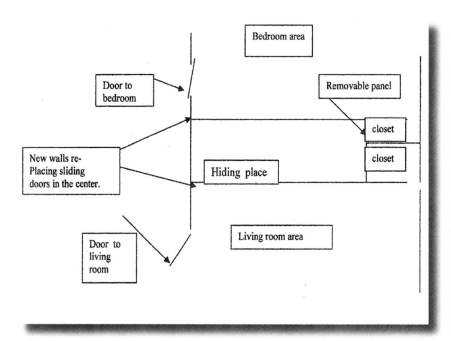

Map of our hiding place

You could only enter the closet from the bedroom. By placing a panel back against the small closet, there was no way to find the entrance to the hiding place. Mr. Thijsen was a very good carpenter, and if anyone looked into the closet, they would not suspect that the inside panel was removable, or that there was a space between the walls. Of course, this was a very small place with standing room only and no light or bathroom facilities.

Maps of WWII Europe and the Netherlands

CHAPTER ONE

Occupation

Amsterdam, May 17, 1940

The invaders have entered Holland and are now in the process of occupying the country.

A little boy stands at the corner, across from the Apollo Skating Rink at the corner of Apollo Avenue in the city of Amsterdam. I really did not know what to do. Should I wave or shout? I was standing there alone at the corner, watching a long line of trucks and armored vehicles carrying German troops.

It seemed vague and difficult to understand.

It was reality, but when you are eight years old many things do not really have much of an impact.

I stood there with my hands on my back for a while, looking at what seemed to be an endless line of trucks of different configurations passing me at a slow speed.

As I stood at that corner, some of the men waved at me. I halfheartedly waved back and then put my hands in my pockets. I looked around to see if anybody was watching me or seen what I had done. I felt I should not have waved at the German soldiers, the enemy.

I decided I had seen enough and walked back to our ground floor apartment, #47, on Apollo Avenue, where I lived with my parents and sister.

The rumble of the trucks went on as I walked back, shaded by the canopy of trees now in bloom.

I wondered if I would have to go to school tomorrow. War seemed to be a nasty thing.

I went back into the apartment, to my room, to play with my Mecano erector set. I thought I would try and build a troop carrier similar to the ones I had seen. I knew I did not have enough parts but thought I would try it anyhow.

Dinner was somewhat quiet. My father was a man quick to create an argument. It seemed that he was never pleased with anything I did. I often wondered if he liked me, even a little, if at all. He was stern and had an easy hand to deal a slap or two with or without reason. That night, I was very surprised what happened during dessert.

He looked at me sternly and said, "I had better show you where we're going to hide the securities."

I looked back at him, totally taken by surprise, and not knowing what securities were, answered somewhat guardedly, "Yes, Dad."

While my sister and mother cleared the table, my father unpacked a small safe about 12x10 and about 5 inches high.

My father, who was not very handy to the point of being somewhat klutzy, tried to open the little safe, but it did not seem to work for him.

"Give it to me," I said, and opened the little safe.

Dad did not say thank you or anything, just took for granted what I did as something he expected.

He showed me the securities. I had never seen them before and was some what impressed by what they seemed to represent.

"They are worth a lot of money, boy, so we don't want them to fall into the hands of the Germans. We will hide them in the cellar."

I nodded in agreement. I had learned not to argue with my dad.

We tried the lock a few more times and felt that it was working properly. Dad proceeded to put the securities into the little safe.

We then got up to go into the cellar, which I had never liked. It was always very dirty. In the winter, I was the one who had to fill up the coal bucket for the living room furnace.

We went down the wooden steps into the cellar. We climbed over the partition where the black coal was kept in the wintertime. There was a hole in the far corner of the wall, which I had never noticed before as it was in the darkest part of the cellar. As I was young and agile, it was easy for me to climb over the waist-high partition. My father, at that time in his early forties, was not too agile and had his difficulties getting into the coal bin, which luckily, was virtually empty at that time because (as planned) we had run out of coal before the summertime.

My father had a hernia that he would not let doctors operate on. He wore a special support to keep the hernia in place. Of course, at that age I did not pay attention to these kinds of things, except I realized it made my father very stiff. If he dropped something on the floor, he would always order me to pick it up, because he did not want to bend over to get it himself.

My father stashed the little safe inside the wall. The builders had failed to close off the wall at that point, leaving a pocket that lent itself to storage of the small safe.

Somehow, I felt that I was part of a conspiracy but did a good job of hiding my excitement, pretending like this seemed to be an everyday occurrence .

Then my father told me to try and see if I could reach the safe. I could and he nodded in satisfaction. He cautioned me to never divulge the hiding place unless he died. If that happened, I was to show it to my mother and/or sister.

At that point, I started to realize that things were much more serious and dangerous than I had ever imagined. The anxiety and tension my father seemed to be under started to penetrate into me like a wave of cold air.

I thought it was best not to tell him that I had waved at the German forces earlier that day, as they had passed our place. My father seemed worried and lost in thoughts of his own. Before climbing out, we surveyed the dusty coal bin and felt it would be impossible for anyone to find the little safe.

We went upstairs to clean the coal dust off our hands and faces. Nothing more was said. I looked for our cat, Snookie. I tried to catch him, but he was too fast for me, so I went back to my room.

As time went on, this little safe almost cost us our lives and caused a number of my family members to be sent to the Auschwitz Concentration Camp, where they were lost forever.

The next days and weeks were spent in quiet exasperation. Basically, everyone we spoke with was trying to outguess what the Germans and Nazis were up to.

Keep in mind that the German military were not so much our concern. Rather, it was the Nazi segment, the Gestapo, and the Sicherheits Dienst (SD) that worried us the most because they were the fanatical killing force that carried out the deaths of 6 million Jews. Of course, in those days, we had no idea what was ahead of us.

My father was of medium height and bald with a fringe of gray hair around the edges of his head. He had a bit of a potbelly and was about forty pounds overweight. His eyes were gray with a tinge of green. His hands were not big, and he kept his fingernails short and clean. At times, he would drive me bananas with his constant cleaning of his fingernails, using the nail of one hand to clean the nails of the other.

Dad did not smile very much, and his demeanor was always serious. You could never see his teeth. He was not a particularly religious man. We only went to temple for very important Jewish holidays such as Yom Kippur. I noticed when we were at temple, he was not too interested in what was going on, but rather, more keen on the business of socializing with the other men in attendance.

Although only in his early forties, exercise was a dirty word in those days and my father was obviously not in good physical shape. He liked to walk but could not swim, and he had a short temper that was often fueled by the attitude and actions of my mother.

I remember that my father loved bones with a lot of marrow in his bowl of soup. He would laboriously hit the bone over his wrist so that the marrow fell out onto a piece of bread. With some salt on it, he would thoroughly enjoy this. There was nothing wrong with this, of course; however, my mother loved to put a bone with no meat or marrow in his bowl. Why, I have no idea, but it would infuriate my father. An argument that lasted at least half an hour would ensue, culminating with my father throwing the bowl of soup at my mother. He never hit her with the bowl, though there were some close misses. Still, my mother would keep on doing this to a point that seemed senseless, and my father would go into a rage about the darn empty bone in his soup bowl.

Looking back on it now, I realize that they were like two little kids annoying each other. The whole thing could have been avoided with my mother giving him a proper bone in his bowl, or my father ignoring the whole thing.

I was very sensitive to these arguments as a kid and I would start to cry. I was not able to deal with the tension that was created. This in turn would anger my father even more, who would then scream at me to stop crying. My mother, I realize, would just do nothing and keep her mouth shut.

To this day, I still do not understand how they managed to annoy each other so much and yet continue to stay married for so long. Sometimes I could only wonder why they stayed together.

How did they find each other? It was quite simple. My mother was a schoolteacher in Enschede, which was located in the eastern part of Holland. Enschede was not big and she became acquainted with my father, who had started a retail store in the center of town. They eventually married and started a family. First came my sister, Ronny, and then me.

We moved to Amsterdam in 1938 where my father started another retail store similar to the one in Enschede. He had sold the first store before we moved to Amsterdam. The store in The Haverstraat Enschede still exists today.

My father would leave early in the morning to go to work at his retail store in the Ferdinand Bolstraat. It was about a twenty-minute walk from where we lived. Though he had a Pontiac sedan, the car was parked in a garage about halfway between the house and the store.

Rubens Het Huis voor Geschenken (Rubens House of Gifts), which measured approximately 1,400 square feet, had an inventory of a variety of merchandise such as handbags, leather goods, luggage, custom jewelry, china, crystal, household goods, giftware, pewter, and other assorted items. The store was always well stocked.

Each day, my mother would take care of the household chores so she could then get to the store as quickly as possible.

She worked there for a couple of reasons. First, she liked it, because she loved to be in sales; but, more importantly, she needed to watch over my father who would flirt with the mostly female clientele. That she did not like. She must have felt that her presence would stop these flirtations.

However, my mother was the best salesperson my father could have had, so he grudgingly let her work in the store.

The cash register rang everything up in cash funds. There were no credit cards or checks and at the end of the workday, my father would put the money from the cash register in his right hip pocket. He was a bit of a show off. Whether appropriate or not, he would flash his bankroll to show that he had a lot of money in his pocket. It must have been something like a security blanket, and it was a great way to impress everybody. He loved to impress people with his worldly ways. He was always able to speak eloquently and had the celebrity aura of an important person. It was an act, but everybody fell for it. Or at least nobody ever questioned him and as it turned out, the cash in his pocket came in handy when we went underground later on.

In a certain way, my mother matched the ways of my dad. She was also overweight by at least forty pounds but kept herself looking good with a corset that was reined in so tight, it played havoc on her digestive system. Not only that, she was easily out of breath as she could not exhale sufficiently. Mom was about five foot three with dark brown hair. Oftentimes, people would remark that she looked a lot like the queen mother of England. Of course, this would please her to no end. She would smile and in feminine fashion, her hand would immediately go to her hair to pat all the curls and make sure they were in the right place. Of course, they always were.

So my father and mother would spend their days in the store. After school, I would arrive at the store, where there was always work for me to do. Deliveries had to be made, which I did on my bicycle if the package was not too big. Boxes and crates had to be unpacked. Merchandise had to be refilled from the storeroom onto the shelves. Difficult packaging of delicate china was thrust into my hands like I was an experienced packaging engineer. I can say, however, that of everything I packed, nothing ever broke. Well, at least I never had a complaint.

I would spend basically all of my spare time in the store or running errands for my father.

I was blessed with dexterity in my hands and often at my young age told to repair things such as cigarette lighters that we sold, or custom jewelry locks or whatever else came around. I had never been taught how to do these things, but usually I was able to figure it out. In those days, things weren't very complex.

At school, I had plenty of problems. Other kids would sometimes harass me. With dark hair, though no pronounced

Jewish features, I was easily pinpointed as Jewish. I actually did not understand at that time the meaning or difference of being Jewish, or what this meant to other people. On the few occasions that I went to temple, everyone there was the same as me. My parents didn't explain this to me, either, so I was at a loss at what to do.

One day, while walking home from school, three older kids ganged up on me and hollered something like "dirty Jew." I had no idea why, because I had never met them. I managed to break loose and run home. That evening at the dinner table I mentioned how some kids I didn't even know, had tried to beat me up and had called me a "dirty Jew."

My dad said, "Ok, let's see if we can find out who they are or where they come from." I was eight years old and definitely not schooled in dirty fighting. I weighed about sixty pounds and didn't have the muscles for schoolyard battle. I don't know if other Jewish kids were harassed. I did not enjoy school very much as the pace of learning seemed very slow and tedious. I was usually already reading the next chapter, while the teacher was still going over old things.

Anyhow, a few days later, late in the day, my dad was home and I pointed out my attackers to him. He gently coached me to lure them into the direction of our place. If they tried to attack me, he would run out of the house and beat them up himself. The plan worked. I half ran back to the house but not very fast and when I was cornered by the three thugs who were ready to beat me up, my father barged through the door to give them hell. They scurried so fast they were gone in a flash. They never showed up again. At that point, I was very proud of my father. It was a side of him I had never seen. The fact that some kids wanted to beat up his son because he was Jewish had really made him mad. I was surprised at that. It was obvious that he wanted to do something about it, and I think he felt pretty good after this little incident.

The French have a saying, "Enfant Terrible," dreadful child, meaning that the kid is a pain in the ass. Or the child is an embarrassment to an adult. I was like that child. Often after dinner if weather permitted, my father and I would go for a walk. During our evening walks, we would meet another fellow or acquaintance on the street and my father would not hesitate to give a cock and bull story that was pure fantasy. I knew the correct story and a couple of times I would say, "But, Dad, you told me it was like this . . ." totally contradicting the story he had just told. It took some educating, but I finally learned not to contradict what my father said. One thing I can say about myself, I learn fast. I learned how to shut up, because I would get a few slaps in the face when we returned home.

I cannot say that there ever was a bond between my father and me. The one thing he lacked was communication skills. I was basically not allowed to say anything unless asked, and had to keep my opinions to myself. Before I even got a chance to voice something, I was told that I was too young to speak for myself, and I should be quiet. My inherent self-confidence was quickly dashed. When I asked my dad a question about something I wanted to know—and, believe me, my curiosity was insatiable—he would tell me to shut up as he looked away from my honest, straightforward stare. I was not supposed to look him in the face but rather, was expected to look down. My mother was present sometimes, but did nothing to mollify the situation. My father was in charge, and that was it.

My sister Ronny was a few years older than me, and we always had a great relationship. She was about five foot two and had beautiful dark brown hair that fell in natural waves. Already at a young age she was developing into a beautiful Rubenesque beauty. (No pun intended as our name is Rubens.) There were plenty of boys coming around the house to see her. She had already developed a great personality, and laughter was her keyword.

It was easy to read my sister's thoughts. Whatever she had on her mind was easily read from her body language and facial expressions. Any emotion was clearly discernible from her face. Actually, she has not changed much over the years; her face still expresses whatever her emotion seems to be at the time. My father could not stand her behavior and she received plenty of negative remarks from him, in which he tried to impress upon her to be more guarded in her ways. However, his remarks made no impression upon my sister; she would not change her ways.

This was the atmosphere in our home when the war broke out and I came out of the cellar with my dad after hiding the little safe.

I continued school, but because I was unable to see what was written on the blackboard, the teacher assigned me to a desk in the front row. Nobody came to the conclusion that: Hey, this kid can't see a damn thing from the back row; maybe he needs glasses. I guess everybody was so involved with the German occupation they didn't have time to worry about an eight year old.

Well, eventually the pressure started around the end of 1940. All Jews were to report to certain German checkpoints to get their ID papers (Ausweisz). If any German caught you without them, you were sent to the eastern front, which is where the war was taking place between Germany and Russia.

If you were sent to the eastern front, you were forced to support the German War Machine. To be sent to the eastern front meant certain death, unless you were able to manage to survive the cold temperatures and subhuman conditions that existed in that area.

At this point, however, we were blissfully and totally unaware of concentration camps even when, unexpectedly, my father was picked up by the Germans. He was held with a few hundred other people, most of who were of some, but not major, importance. Why, nobody knew. My father was able to get a short-penciled note off to us and after about ten days was told he could go home. While my father was gone, my mother did not seem to do anything at all. She was at a loss. I was actually too young to understand what was really going on, but my mother did not seem to be able to explain it to us, either.

We waited patiently, hoping my father would come back soon.

When he returned, he complained bitterly that they had everybody do physical exercise in the morning. To the best of my knowledge, physical exercise in those days was a foreign word. At this point, my father's attitude about the Germans changed drastically. I believe he had now become fearful for our lives.

As a young man in his twenties, my father worked and lived for a number of years in Germany. He learned window

31

dressing for store window displays. Of course, he spoke the German language fluently. Eventually, he went back to Enschede, across the border in Holland, where his parents were living at that time.

When he came back from his incarceration, he had a good idea what the Nazis were up to and started to understand the attitude of the Germans.

I believe it was in late 1940 that my father lost his retail store located at 106-108 Ferdinand Bolstraat in Amsterdam.

My father was standing in his store behind the cash register, which allowed him to overlook both sides of the store, when a man walked in with a German soldier carrying a rifle. The man addressed my father as follows: "Jew Rubens, get your coat and get the hell out. I am taking possession of your store. You are out. So, get going."

My father was allowed to get his overcoat and barely time to get his hat and was actually booted out of the store by the soldier and the man who had gotten himself appointed by German authorities to take over my father's retail store. Needless to say, whatever money was in the cash register was taken as well.

His bank account was immediately blocked. The Verwalter, as these people were called by the Germans, simply took possession. Here, the Verwalter was a Dutch person who went to the Germans and explained that he had knowledge of a Jewish-owned store or business that he would like to take over.

The Germans supported this and the Jewish owner, in this case, my father, was kicked out of his business in an instant.

My father's incarceration, the stealing of his retail store, and his experiences in Germany as a young man served as a wake-up-call. He now had a clearer idea what might be in store for him and many other people.

He had already taken steps to convert the majority of his holdings into cash, sizeable amounts of which he carried with him most of the time. Early in 1940 my dad had already lost his car. A 1939 Pontiac. I had only one desire and that was to drive that car myself, although I was already happy with my job of turning the turn signals on and off.

With the car gone, the store gone, and no work to do, my father seemed uncertain about what to do next.

We muddled on for a number of weeks. Rumors started to filter in that the Germans were picking up Jewish people all over the place, and they were being sent to a place in the northern part of Holland called Westerbork, a concentration/holding camp.

Although not known at the time, from there, people were transported in cattle cars to the dreaded concentration camps in East Germany and Poland.

The Germans were willing to shoot a person without really giving it much thought. In fact, it was shoot first and then perhaps ask questions later.

Razzia (raid) was quickly a word we all recognized as meaning that the Germans had hauled off people for incarceration or they were being sent to Westerbork, the now dreaded concentration camp in the province of Drente. Simply put, Razzia also meant that the Germans would block off an area with military precision so nobody could slip away.

You could smell the fear in the air. Everybody was looking over their shoulders, not knowing from where the next calamity might come.

Though my father had no car, he started making numerous trips to the grocery stores and other resources to stock up on food. I remember he once found a cache of about a 150 cans of tomato soup with rice. We ate it so often that fifty years later I'm still hesitant to have tomato soup and/or rice.

Food was pretty much a major concern for everybody, especially when we had to buy it with little vouchers the size of postage stamps, which was another system by which the Germans would exercise control over the population. Without the little vouchers, it became virtually impossible to buy food.

CHAPTER TWO

Underground

One day, I believe in September of 1941, my father came into my room and said: "Put on about three sets of underwear and an extra sweater. We're going underground, but we can't take any luggage with us because that could look suspicious. It will have to look like we're just going for a walk."

When I asked where we were going, he mumbled that we were going to Westeinde Street.

That afternoon my dad and I walked to the Westeinde, which took us about forty-five minutes. As we were never very close, there was little to no conversation.

Oftentimes, I felt that my dad disliked me. It was only in later years that I came to understand what he went through and believed he behaved this way toward me because his upbringing was not very pleasant. Conversely, he may have felt that the only way for me to survive was through trial and error and to find out things for myself. I also believe he was a bad communicator because it seemed difficult for him to have a conversation with an eight year old. That eight year old could ask more questions than ten professors could answer, my father would complain.

I was blessed with an insatiable curiosity and an intensity to check things out.

So, here we were at the Westeinde (Westend Street) in a small 8'x8' bedroom. Two windows from which we could look out showed the roof of a quasi-shopping gallery with a glass roof, which was either very dirty or made in such a way that you couldn't see through it much less see the people walking below in the "Gallery," as it was called. But then, the few times that I was able to venture out, I noticed that it was never really very busy in the Gallery.

So, here we sat in this small bedroom. I had stopped asking my dad questions because he would not respond to them anyhow. I had no toys with me of course, and while my metal Mecano erector set would have kept me busy for hours, I had not been permitted to bring it with me. As there were no cooking facilities, we ate some bread and drank water.

Around 10:00 p.m., on that first night, I woke up and asked my dad where the toilet was. Unceremoniously, he pointed at the washbasin in the room and told me to stand on a chair. Ok. Why not, I said to myself as I used the washbasin to relieve myself, rinsing it out very thoroughly with the water faucet when finished.

We spent a few days in that room. While there, I was introduced to Mrs. Eusman, who rented the space to my dad. She was a tall, skinny woman with a face that seemed to express no emotion at any time. Her salt-and-pepper-colored hair was combed into a short pageboy. She wore no makeup, said very little, and her demeanor seemed to be simple and to the point. Her clothing was drab and dark in color. Her face showed few lines because she never smiled. She was in her late forties, about five foot eight, and seemed to me to be a giant.

After about five more days, my mother and sister arrived at our hiding place. Meanwhile, my father had made arrangements with Mrs. Eusman for more space.

I had a little room for myself, about 5'x7', with a window that looked out over the Gallery. I was supposed to stay away from the windows so that nobody would notice that anyone was in our rooms, although the thin window coverings made it impossible for anybody to see into the room from the outside.

Our living room was about 9'x10' with sliding doors that opened up to my parents' bedroom, which was similar in size. A hallway ran along the side of these two rooms that connected to a small kitchen with limited facilities. Also off the hallway was a small room that was just big enough for a toilet and a tiny sink in which you could wash your hands. If you sat down and leaned forward just a little, your head would touch the door. At each end of the hallway were two small bedrooms like mine. So we had a 3-bedroom apartment with a sitting room and a small kitchen.

In the living room were two windows separated from each other by a 3' foot solid wall space. Across the street was a bar and restaurant that never seemed to be busy. To the left was a bridge leading over a canal. It was only a short distance from there to the Albert Cuyp open air market, where, before the war, I would go from time to time to treat myself to French fries. To go there now, however, was out of the question.

To get to our hiding place, you had to walk up two flights of stairs that had a small landing in between. We lived on the second floor, actually, because the apartments were built over or above the Gallery. From the front living room, we looked out over the street. There was also a window in the bedroom that looked out over the Gallery.

At nighttime, before we turned on the lights, all windows were blacked out—not for the Germans, but so that the planes flying over from England to bomb Germany would not be able to see anything. At night, you could not see a glimmer of light anywhere. Cars driven at night—that is, the few cars allowed to be driven—had special hooding over the headlights, which supposedly made them "invisible" from the air.

Since Holland is east of Germany, the blackout idea was meant to ensure that the planes from England had no reference point as they flew over to Germany to drop their loads of bombs.

Mrs. Eusman lived alone on the third floor of the apartment building. We soon learned that there was a fourth floor space where another couple lived. The man was Polish, but we never figured out where the woman with him came from. I often visited them. He was always dressed in a T-shirt and trousers. I forgot his name. He was rather muscular and was bald headed. They were quiet people and kept to themselves. The woman was somewhat sexy looking with dark hair and a nice figure, but she dressed like a slob and spent most of her time in her nightclothes.

The radio was always playing in their apartment, which might have been the attraction for me to go there. I was bored and they seemed to welcome my visits. As it turned out, we were in a house totally rented out to people in hiding from the Germans.

The days passed by. We would sneak looks through the thin curtains to see what was happening down on the street. We had an illegal radio and listened to the clandestine BBC. Every word from the BBC was like a lifeline of hope, giving indications of what was happening outside and beyond the Netherlands. My father had a map of Europe and Africa, and we would look for hours to locate a particular city or village. Watching the Allied war efforts gave us a feeling that we had a chance to survive. We paid close attention to whatever was going on outside the Netherlands, as that was an indication of what might be headed our way.

We also listened to music on the radio. One night my sister taught me how to dance the foxtrot. For once, a jazz band was playing halfway nice music and we were dancing before we knew it. Somehow I picked up on how to do the foxtrot in just a few minutes.

I have never forgotten that time. Thanks to my sister, I became a pretty good dancer.

People from the Underground forces, that helped people like us with food vouchers and information, would visit us approximately every two weeks, keeping us informed about what was going on in the Netherlands.

The picture was an unhappy one. All we heard was that the Germans were finding people and either sending them to work camps, concentration camps, or shooting them on sight if they tried to escape. It was a grim picture.

Life became monotonous.

We got up in the morning, ate breakfast, and sat around and talked, not really doing anything. We listened to the BBC, marked the map on the wall where the Allies were, and noted what was happening on the different fronts.

We would then have a simple lunch in the afternoon. Again, not doing much, but perhaps just listening to the local radio stations, which carried classical music and German propaganda. When Hitler spoke, we sat glued to the radio to hear him scream and listened as thousands of people shouted *Heil, Hitler*. My German wasn't that good, but my father understood every word and his face would grow pale with anxiety. It seemed to make our situation even more desperate.

For me, school was out of the question. Now and then I would get a book to read. But, for the most part, my education was totally halted.

Twice a week, and always at nighttime, I can remember that Dad and I would venture outside for a walk, never very far, and usually to pick up food of some sort. We had found a clandestine bakery where we could pick up some fantastic whole-wheat pumpernickel. It tasted so good; I could eat it without anything on it. Or we would walk over to see Mr. Thijssen, the carpenter who lived only a few blocks away.

Mr. Thijssen, a member of the Underground, was a tall man with black hair. He had a lovely family. His wife was a very caring person and I loved being there. Their daughter was a few years older than I and invariably; I would end up in her room (although I don't really remember now what we did). She always showed a great deal of interest in me.

We did not hug or anything like that, but, somehow we surreptitiously seemed to touch each other, both being so young and confused. It was nice, warm, and cozy. On a cold night, we would sit close together while the grown-ups talked about the war and the raids executed by the Germans; we shared some togetherness. That companionship seemed to warm the soul and made us feel good. (I wish I could remember her name.) Just to spend some time with someone close to my age was a wonderful thing.

Meanwhile, Mr. Thijssen came up with a plan to create a hiding place, within our hiding place.

His idea was to build two walls where the sliding doors separated the living room from the bedroom so that one could enter the 3.5' wide space by removing the entire wooden side panel inside the adjoining wall closet, which likewise adjoined the hiding place.

You could only enter the closet from the bedroom.

By placing the panel back against the small closet inside the hiding place, there was no way to find an entrance into the hiding place. If anyone looked in the closet, they would never suspect that the inside panel on the right was removable, or that there was a space between the walls in which to hide.

Everyone agreed that the two walls should be built. Now if there was a raid and the Germans went from door to door, we could go into the hiding place. Unless a person knew where it was, they would never otherwise notice it. Mr. Thijssen was a very good carpenter.

It would seem that nobody could find this hiding place. It could be compared to a magician's double wall. Of course, there were no lights or facilities in this small space. Not even room to sit down.

The idea of hiding there while Germans searched the premises almost scared everybody out of their minds. We only hoped we would never have to use it.

My father thought it would also be a good place to hide the little safe we had originally stashed away behind the coal bin. My mother had brought it along when it was no longer safe to go to our old place at the Apollolaan. So now it rested on the floor at the far end of our new hiding place. From time to time, I would enter that hiding place and sit there, fantasizing or thinking about music.

I would imagine that I was standing in front of a gigantic orchestra, directing its various sections.

I could hear the music in my mind. Just thinking about it and how the orchestra would play, it must have calmed me and kept me sane and at peace with myself. At night when I went to bed, before falling asleep, the same thing would happen. It seemed there was always music going through my head. I had no instrument on which to play. I just had to use my imagination. When you are eight years old, imagination knows no boundaries or limitations.

44

My father often rented movies through the mail—Charlie Chaplin, Oliver and Hardy, the Keystone Cops, and so many others—and we shared them with everybody in the house. Once a week, we had what became known as entertainment night—usually on Saturdays—and what a delight they were! We had a projector and a screen. And I don't know why, but it just seemed natural that tending to and focusing the projector, spooling the films, setting up the screen, and repairing breaks in the old, often brittle film (and there were plenty), fell to me. I was the one in charge—the one who seemed to always know exactly what to do. Nobody had to show me; it seemed so easy, I just figured it all out by myself. Oh, I remember those evenings as though they were only yesterday.

But, wait . . . let me backtrack for a moment.

My father had two brothers, Uncle Harry and Uncle Mozes. Uncle Harry was married to a Christian lady, my Aunt Corry. By virtue of their "mixed" marriage, Uncle Harry and Aunt Corry were in far less danger than a married couple who were both Jewish. Therefore, my Uncle Harry's family did not hide from the Nazis, and they all survived the war.

But, there was a problem. Uncle Harry was hiding his mother (my Grandma), his sister, her daughter, and Uncle Mozes. Since it was determined that it was far too dangerous for them to stay at their own place, they all moved in with us.

The logistics of food, sleeping, and eight people being together in a small area was a test beyond anything any of us had ever experienced before. Fortunately, we realized we all had to get along with each other, so the only tension was from our fear of the Nazis. By now, we knew if we were caught, we would be finished. Even though I was only eight years old, I was fully aware of the situation we faced and knew, for example, that playing outside in the street was suicidal.

Dad and I still went out a couple of times a week, always at night, foraging for food. Today I remember well those frosty, full moon nights. We would walk in the shadows as much as possible, enjoying being outside for maybe an hour at the most. Dad would hardly say anything. The walks were quiet. We were always watchful of our surroundings. There were no streetlights because of the blackouts; so unless there was moonlight, the streets were very dark.

Luckily, we never ran into any Germans and we returned to the apartment, somewhat cold but pleased with our foraging of dark brown bread from the clandestine baker.

There was no shower or tub in the apartment. Once a week we would boil water to pour into a big tub-like container, which was too small for me to sit in but I could give myself a sponge bath, which may be why I now love a Jacuzzi or plain hot bath.

In the wintertime, it could get pretty chilly in the apartment. It was heated but not sufficiently enough to keep all of the rooms warm. Therefore, taking a bath would really be a chilly undertaking! I would stand there shivering like a leaf in the wind, in my naked nothing.

From time to time, Christians from the Underground Movement would visit and bring us food vouchers. Extensive coffee preparations would ensue to warm our visitors who were our only link to the outside world. Besides the vouchers, we hung on to every word they said and on the information they provided concerning what had been happening in the city, what the Germans were doing, and who had disappeared. Betrayal was the order of the day. As an incentive, the Nazis offered money to anybody who could tell them where to find the "Jews." Their determination was fanatic and consistent, fueled by speeches of Adolf Hitler and his propaganda machine.

Because the only individuals who knew about our hiding place was Mrs. Eusman and two people from the Underground Movement, we felt very secure in our cocoon. We were paying rent and, therefore, had complete trust in our landlady. The Underground people were totally dedicated to assisting us. Of course, there was also Mr. Thijssen, the carpenter, who had built our hiding place, but his trust was beyond question.

One morning, without warning, hundreds of soldiers, trucks, machine guns, and plainclothes SD held a raid that was stopped just at the bridge that we could see from the front window. We watched the proceedings and saw a number of people being hauled out of their houses and thrown into trucks to be sent to concentration camps or prisons. You could cut the tension in our apartment with a knife. If they crossed the bridge and went door to door, we would hide in the hiding place Mr. Thijssen had built for us. We sat there for about five hours, waiting to see what would happen, and wondering if they would cross the bridge.

Everybody felt strangely detached about the poor unfortunate people who had been caught during the raid. We felt bad for them but, of course, we were relieved that it wasn't us. We were silently praying that they would not cross the bridge, and ultimately they didn't. After many hours of tension, they left and we started to count our blessings.

After the war, we estimated that for about 800.00 Dutch guilders, or approximately $250.00, someone betrayed us. And that someone was Mrs. Eusman who ultimately sold us out to the Nazis.

It was about 8:30 p.m. or so when the doorbell rang. I was in the hallway, and I remember Mrs. Eusman running down one flight of stairs from her floor, which in and of itself was unusual, and pulling on the rope that opened the door two flights down. Two men in raincoats ran up the stairs at great speed, and one of them said, "SD!! You Jews all go in that room."

They acted swiftly. Everybody was terror stricken, as if our breath had been taken away from us. Paralyzed, we moved zombie-like into the living room and listened to their instructions about what and what not to do.

Uncle Mozes was in the toilet when the two SD policemen ran up the stairs. As we were herded into the living room, I saw him sneak out and down the hallway in gingerly fashion. He managed to escape with just the clothes on his back. He made it through the war. After the war, I visited with him from time to time. He was a kind man and I remember him well.

While we were herded into the living room, one of the SD thugs went directly to the hiding place, triumphantly picking up the little safe with the securities off the floor.

At that point, we realized who had betrayed us to the Nazis. It could only have been Mrs. Eusman. I don't know what happened to the securities after we were taken away. Perhaps they were split between various parties.

The table from which I showed the movies on Saturday nights sat in the center of the living room. My father was standing at the end of the table, his back towards the windows.

I was standing directly behind him, perhaps trying to hide from the SD police.

As noted earlier, my father always carried large sums of money in his pocket. Since I was standing behind him, I noticed that he had taken the money out of his hip pocket and was gesturing for me to take it from him, although it took me a few seconds to realize that's what he wanted me to do. As I think back on it now, he must have been absolutely petrified that the SD would notice what he was doing.

I took the money out of his hands and quickly tucked it inside my shirt, where the bulge would not be quite as noticeable. We were told to get warm clothes, toiletries, and other bare necessities. Whatever money or valuables we had were taken from us. However, a little kid, eight or nine years old, is not supposed to have money on him, so I was never searched or questioned. I managed to keep the sizable bundle of money hidden under my shirt until my father felt it was safe for him to take it back. As it turned out, it was a considerable sum of money that virtually carried us all through the war.

A car, best described as a paddy wagon, pulled up to the curb and we were all bundled into the back and taken to what was called the Jewish Theater (now a museum) on the Plantage Middellaan, which had been converted to a holding place for Jewish people collected over a period of time.

The chairs in the center were pushed to the sides and at night, people slept on the floor with their meager belongings. Everybody had what was considered his or her own little square.

My sister and I were separated from our parents. Across the street was a building where all the children were held. Every afternoon we were herded across the street so we could visit with our parents for about half an hour and then we were taken back to the "Crèche," as it was called. We slept and ate there and were biding our time until we were transported to the Westerbork concentration camp, which while transitional was also known as the camp many never left throughout the war.

Unbeknownst to me, one day my sister found a way to escape from the Creche through an unlocked exit door. Since it was a matter of survival, she merely opened the door that day and walked away. I did not know for several days following her departure that she had done so.

While in the Creche, separated from our parents, we did simple things to enjoy ourselves. For example, I remember there was a pole lamp standing on the floor, off to the side of the room, rather than in the way of foot traffic. It was already dark outside so somebody had turned on the lamp by plugging it into a wall socket. I decided to move the lamp closer to the wall to ensure that nobody would fall over it. I grabbed the pole with both hands to lift it. It turned out there was a short in the lamp and the metal pole and the metal had the full force of 240 going through it. I was being electrocuted. I was paralyzed in my hands and could not let go of the pole! Involuntarily, with my legs still working, I somehow managed to walk backwards, pulling the plug out of the wall socket. I could barely breathe or talk. Nobody had noticed anything, and I was afraid to say anything for fear of being punished.

After about an hour, I recovered. I never told my parents what had happened. However, I became very wary around electrical equipment, a fear that remains with me to this day. In the days following the incident with the pole lamp, I wanted desperately to get out of the holding area, but there was no escape.

Meanwhile, my father had managed to bribe a German soldier. So, the plan was when the trucks came to transport everybody to the railway station, the soldier would release the rope that held the heavy canvas covering on the truck in place. My parents were to jumped off the truck. Because the street was not very wide, there were no guards on that side of the truck.

Wanting to get me out as well, Dad told me to grab all of my belongings and take them with me to the Theater because otherwise we were all going to Westerbork. Although I was not really certain what that meant, I did know that it was not a good thing to be locked up in a concentration camp. When I got to the Theater, my father coached me as follows: "Listen carefully," he said. "I have arranged with a member of the Jewish Council for you to go back to the Creche. You pretend you left your sweater behind and would like to take it with you. That man over there," he said, pointing to an individual standing nearby, "Will take you across. When you get half way across the street, start running as fast as you can. He will not follow you because he can't run as fast as you can. So, just run away and continue running until you get to Mr. Thijssen's. Do you understand?"

I nodded, indicating that I had heard everything my father   said. He then walked over to the man he had pointed out to me. "Please," my father said, "would you take my son across to the Creche? He left his sweater behind." The man nodded and said, "Yeah, sure. He'll need warm clothes, I'll take him across." The man took me by the hand and proceeded to the front door. There were a number of doors, all of them heavily guarded. He said something to a German soldier, indicating that he would return with me in a few minutes.

We started crossing the street, which had a double railway track for the streetcars that passed by. On each side of the street was a pedestrian island.

When we reached the first island, I pulled my hand

out of his and started running as fast as I could. I ran towards the City Zoo, fully expecting to lose myself in some side street. I had barely turned the corner when I heard a voice screaming behind me, "Halt! Halt! Halt!" I also heard the sound of hobnailed boots pounding on the sidewalk.

At that point, I knew that a German soldier was very close behind me. Fear, total devastating fear started taking over my senses, and I started to lose control of my legs, which seemed to have turned into jelly.

I could not control my legs any longer and literally fell to the pavement, unable to stand. Before I fell to the ground completely, however, which seemed to happen in almost slow motion, the soldier grabbed my arm, pulled me up, and dragged me back to the Creche. I was shaken, crying, fearful, and totally in a state of panic, not knowing what to do. I knew that this had been my chance to escape. I did not know if I would have another one.

My thinking process was totally out of order. All I could do was cry, which I fortunately managed to control after a while. I must have sat at the door inside the Creche for about forty minutes. Unbeknownst to me, my father saw everything that had happened. He had not expected that a soldier would chase me. Luckily, the soldier brought me back to the Creche, not to the Theater, because there was little to no security in the Creche.

When my father realized what had happened, he begged the Jewish Board to figure out a way to get me out of the Creche.

Next to the entrance of the Creche was a door, about fifteen feet to the side of the main entrance. As my sister explained to me much later, this was the same door she had found and made good her escape. Tearfully, sitting just inside the lobby of the Creche, I was approached by a man from the Jewish Advisory Board, who simply said, "Come with me."

He then took me by the hand, leading me through two corridors I had never noticed before. He opened a door, and said, "Just walk out slowly and quietly, and don't look back." I did exactly what he said. I walked out and strolled away from the Creche, covering the Star of David with my sweater nonchalantly flung over my shoulder. No one took notice of a little kid.

CHAPTER THREE

To the
Next Hiding Place

I walked leisurely down the street away from the Theater. I controlled myself from running, knowing that to do so would only draw attention to me.

I walked aimlessly for about fifteen minutes, trying to figure out how to get to Mr. Thijssen's.

As I walked, I stopped at a bridge spanning a canal and leaned over the railing. At the same time, with one hand under my sweater covering the Star of David, I was trying to tear the yellow patch off my jacket. It took me quite a while because my mother had sewn it on very well. Finally, I got the yellow star off my jacket and crumpled it into a little ball and threw it off the bridge into the water. Boy, what a relief that was! With the star on my jacket, I could have easily been picked up just for walking on the street.

I must have walked for a couple of hours, as I was a little bit lost and still shaken by my ordeal with the German soldier, but finally found my way and rang the bell at Mr. Thijssen's residence.

The door opened and I was welcomed with open arms. My sister was already there. We were now waiting to see if our parents would also make it to the safe house.

They arrived safely that evening and told us how they had been able to escape. Sadly, however, my grandmother, her daughter, and her granddaughter were sent to Westerbork, and then to Auschwitz immediately thereafter. I did not learn until 1997 that upon their arrival in Auschwitz, they were sent directly to the gas chambers.

Following their arrival late that evening, my father and mother told us the following story:

During their involuntary stay at the Theater, my father, with his fluency of the German language, acquainted himself with a German soldier/guard. Dad spun a tale that he had stuffed some diamonds in the side of an easy chair at the apartment where we had been hiding. He managed to talk the guard into taking him to that apartment. Prior to that, he had taken a diamond ring that my mother had kept hidden on her and when he was at the apartment he palmed the diamond ring and gave it to the guard under the guise that he had actually pulled it out of the side of the easy chair. So there were two reasons to get to the hiding place: to see if anything could be salvaged while there, and to establish the bribe with the German guard.

Everything seemed to go according to plan. After I managed to escape, my parents were anxious to escape as well. The plan was still to flee from the transport truck.

Under heavy guard, they were loaded into the trucks covered with canvas. My mother went straight to the left rear of the truck to check if the canvas was removable or sufficiently loose. She found that it was. The German soldier that my father had bribed had kept his word. Without further delay, she said to my dad, "Let's jump out of here," and they did.

As my mother jumped out, a streetcar came along on her side with the doors open, and she stepped right in—like it was planned. At the same time, my father stepped between the tandem car of the streetcar to place himself on the other side of the street. A number of people in the streetcar saw them jump from the truck, but none of them said a word. The driver took off within seconds like he was part of the plot that had my mother stepping into the streetcar. My father, noting that my mother was safe, gently scurried away through the darkened streets. Both were now on their way to the Thijssen apartment and safe house.

It is interesting to recall now that when we got together, there was no hugging, crying, or hand holding. No prayer of thanks—just a nod and, "Oh, I'm so glad you made it." Warmth seemed totally lacking in our household, or in our family in general. It seemed like everybody was scared to show any emotion. Whatever happened was dealt with in a matter of fact way with perhaps the only exception being that there was a fair amount of joking and jesting. At least there was a fair amount of laughter. Perhaps the tension we were under was so severe, everybody was afraid to drop their guard. Afraid to break down. Keeping up a front of strength. We all did and succeeded admiringly well. It was not that everybody was telling jokes. It was more a matter of lightheartedness. Poking fun at things in general.

Perhaps it was the laughter that kept us sane from all the pressure and tension. In later years, I must admit that laughter was one of the greatest medicines to keep things in balance. Even laughing at oneself seemed to clear the mind of pressure and anxiety. Heads up and smile was the order of the day. It was an act, but it helped to hide our fears and desperation.

As it turned out, we could not stay at the Thijssen place because he was part of the Underground and had to keep a low profile. It was simply too dangerous.

So we found a place at the Admiral de Ruyterweg. The apartment was not spacious, and it was a temporary thing. I don't remember the name of our landlady, but I do recall that she had a big smile on her face most of the time. She was roly-poly and about fifty pounds overweight. When we had dinner, my mother would try to be thrifty and save something for the next day. However, our landlady would laugh and say, "Oh, let's just finish it. A bomb could hit us tonight. Let's enjoy it while we can." So we ate quite well at the Admiral de Ruyterweg. Despite my efforts since then, I have never been able to find that apartment again because all of the apartments on that street seem to look the same.

I did not have many clothes. All I had were a pair of short pants, one or two shirts, a few pairs of underwear, and one pair of shoes. The weather was starting to turn cooler. The heating had not yet been turned on. My legs always seemed to be cold, and I found myself hugging them to stay warm.

Well, under those conditions, it was a given that I would become violently ill. I had very high fever but did not know what I was suffering from. Whatever it was, it was so serious that a doctor had to be called in.

I remember looking at the doctor and seeing him through a haze. I felt so tired. I couldn't move a muscle. I think my mother must have spoon fed me because I couldn't even lift my little finger.

I never found out what was really wrong with me, but it seemed that one morning I just woke up and suddenly felt fine. At that point, I felt some warmth from both my parents who, of course, were tremendously relieved that I had recovered. During that period, I don't recall seeing my sister. I think she was kept away from me because everybody was afraid that my illness could be contagious.

My sister Ronny and I always got along well. While we were underground, she would often come to me with a comb and brush and ask me to brush her hair, which was chestnutbrown. It had a beautiful glow to it and was very thick. Sometimes it was a heavy job. I always felt good afterwards; tired, yes, but also good.

My sister was also quite Rubenesque, for lack of a better descriptive word. Although young, she was very well developed. As she had a difficult time hooking her bra herself, the task fell to me every morning. At least that's how she explained it to me. Fortunately, our relationship was not marred by anything. Often, of course, we only had each other, so in many ways, it was obvious that we would gravitate toward each other for support.

So, the time came to leave Amsterdam. By now, it was early 1943. For safety reasons, the Underground had made arrangements for us to split up. My parents were going to live with an elderly lady in a villa near Utrecht, under the guise of being refugees from the south of Holland.

My father's facial expressions were usually serious and unsmiling. Give him a uniform and he'd pass for an officer. Straight nose, glasses—definitely no Jewish looks at all.

My mother had short dark brown hair and could easily pass for being from the south. My father's name was Paul Jacques Rubens, but was now changed to Henk Brouwer. My mother's name, originally Evelyn, was now Marie. My name, originally Sallo, became Jan (John). My sister's name was changed to Annie Vogel.

As I became older, I began to dislike my name. The word *salot* in French means dirty son-of-a-bitch—which for obvious reasons is not a good name to use when you deal or travel with the French. Because the pronunciation of my name, *Sallo* in French almost sounds the same as *salot*, I later officially changed my name to Stan.

So, armed with my new identity, I was asked to go with a smiling gentleman, Uncle Kees, who came to pick me up. Uncle Kees stood at about five foot five, without an ounce of fat on him. He had thinning hair and was about forty-five years old. In his own way, he tried to put me at ease. Before the war, he had been a chauffeur for another uncle of mine. Now he was a security guard. He lived with his wife Dien and their four-year-old son, Adje, in a small two-bedroom apartment in the Bandoeng straat in Utrecht, in the middle of Holland, not far from the railway station.

We took the train from Grand Central Station out of Amsterdam to Utrecht and walked from the station to the apartment where I would live for the next ten months of my life. To my delight, when we arrived at the apartment, my cousin Andre was also there.

Andre's mother and sister had been with us when we were betrayed in Amsterdam by Mrs. Eusman. Andre had no idea about the fate of his sister and mother. Of course, nobody else did, either. Andre was about fifteen years old at that time. Totally pleasant in every way. He had a bit of a hooked nose, dark hair and was much taller then me, but then we were both still growing.

64

Our world consisted of a living room, my aunt and uncle's bedroom, which they shared with Adje, a hallway connecting all rooms to our bedroom, the kitchen, and a toilet room. Andre and I slept in a bed that was just a little bit larger than an atypical single bed. Because Andre suffered badly from asthma, I awoke on many nights because he was having trouble breathing. I would have given anything to have been able to make it easier for him to breath.

From our bedroom, we could open a door to a small balcony about 3.5' deep that connected to a door into the kitchen. Whenever we went to the balcony, we made sure not to raise our heads above the railing. We knew that nobody could or should see us at any cost. Usually, I was on hands and knees when I was on the balcony.

The floor of the balcony was made of lead, which was icy cold in the winter and burning hot during the summer.

One day, everybody had left the apartment except, of course, Andre and me. When we were left alone, we would walk around the apartment very carefully, just to make sure nobody on the lower floor knew there was anybody above them. Even conversation was kept to a minimum. We were well trained to be very quiet. However, on this particular day, I had to use the bathroom. We would not flush the toilet when we were by ourselves. In a reflex movement, however,

I accidentally pulled the chain to flush the toilet, realizing immediately what I had done.

I crept out of the toilet room, quiet as a mouse, scared out of my wits that I had given us away. For hours, I sat in a corner doing nothing, waiting for somebody to knock on the door, but nothing happened. Apparently, the flushing of a toilet is such a normal thing, nobody had paid any attention to it.

Because the Bandoeng straat was not very wide, you could almost see into the windows or rooms of the people across the street. Of course, we stayed away from the windows so nobody could see us. It seems that across the street, a few numbers down, there were some people, either living underground or in a similar situation as us, hiding from the Nazis. On this particular day, it was about 9:00 a.m.

Razzia!

Within maybe only a minute, the entire street was blocked on all sides.

Nowhere to go, except maybe up to the roof. That, of course, was not safe, especially in the daylight. We got the impression that only one apartment was targeted by the Nazi police.

A number of people were arrested. Uncle Kees looked out the window and reported what was going on. How did they know there were people hiding there? Obviously, somebody had tipped off the Germans. They had been betrayed, and I knew how they felt. It was so clear to us that we, too, were in constant danger of being arrested by the Nazis.

During the day, Andre and I tried to keep ourselves occupied. Aunt Dien had been able to get some English language study books. So Andre, with the help of the books, was teaching me English. At the same time he was tutoring me, he was learning the language, too. We needed some kind of diversion. We never went out. We always stayed within the few rooms of the apartment. Sometimes I would just lay on the floor or get up and listen to what was called "Radio Hilversum #1 and #2." The music played was not very compelling to listen to; and the news was strictly propaganda and did not tell us anything worthwhile, because they were German-controlled radio stations. So, my eyes devoured whatever books I could lay my hands on.

But, then, we also had our *castle* to play with, which Andre and I constructed from wooden cigar boxes.

It had an imaginary moat, because we had made a drawbridge that hinged up and down by means of a winding contraption we had created. To shape the various parts to fit together, as we were building the castle, we rubbed the pieces we had cut with a sharp-bladed knife. A red brick served as sandpaper. We had glue, which was called Velpon, but no nails. Luckily, the glue was available and not costly.

Diligently, we worked for weeks creating our castle. Perhaps in our subconscious minds, the castle represented a safe haven where nobody could penetrate our defenses. Uncle Kees was able to get us the empty cigar boxes. The wood was about an eighth of an inch thick. It was great fun working with it. We would cut the pieces to an exact shape and then sand it down on the brick to an exacting finish so the glue would stick where it was supposed to. For hours we worked on the castle and, when finished, we had our fun with it for many months to come.

Word got out that the Germans were holding raids all over the place to get young men for their labor camps. Although these were different from concentration camps, nobody wanted to go to work for the German forces. Those that were picked up were housed in barracks of about forty people. The accommodations were terrible and the food was even worse. Unlike the concentration camps, the conditions were not life-threatening, but they were very, very grim nonetheless.

As a kid, I really wasn't in danger. On the other hand, Andre, who was now about sixteen years old, *was* in danger, especially if the Germans went from door to door in our area. Therefore, our guardians decided to arrange for temporary space for Andre with Aunt Dien's family, who lived further out of town.

Now the question was how to get Andre safely there. Solution? Dress him like a woman, which is what we did. Aunt Dien came up with all kinds of clothes and managed to make them fit, including a pair of her high-heeled shoes. He wore a hat to cover his hair, a dress that hung down to his knees, and even a necklace. However, we passed on making him wear earrings.

While Andre got dressed in the clothes, we watched from the hallway, laughing so hard we could hardly stand. In the end, even with the limited items we had available, rouge on his cheeks, powdered nose and face, he really did manage to look like a woman.

He ultimately arrived safely a Aunt Dien's family place, riding on the back of a bicycle complete with wooden tires. Yes, wooden tires. Because actual bicycle tires were not available, they were made out of little pieces of wood that were held together with wire.

Thinking back on it now, to this day I do not like to dress up in costume. As much as I enjoy watching what other people wear, Halloween is wasted on me, I suppose primarily because it brings back too many unhappy memories about the war.

Eventually, after the possibility of raids in our area had passed, Andre was able to return to us, pretty much dressed the same way he was when he left, right down to sitting on the back of a bicycle with wooden tires.

CHAPTER FOUR

Another Raid and Another Close Call

The days came and went and for a while, everything was reasonably quiet. Then, one evening in October of 1943 the Nazis staged another raid and we were faced with the question of where to hide. If we were caught in the apartment, Aunt Dien and Uncle Kees would most likely lose their lives as well. Since we had never been on the roof, it was decided that Andre and I would go up there to hide. It was very dark. The temperature was around 42 degrees and a cold, numbing wind was blowing.

From the lead inlaid balcony, we climbed the stepladder leaning against the brick wall. From the top of the wall, we thought we would be able to stand on its ridge and than pull ourselves up, onto the roof.

As I climbed the ladder, I expected to see another balcony adjoining ours on the other side of the brick wall, but I was wrong because on the other side of the wall was a sheer, three-story drop. The totally dark and empty space made me almost lose my balance and fall to the ground.

There was virtually nothing to hold on to, except the outside wall of the apartment building. We still had to climb onto and along the 7-8" wide skinny ledge of the red brick wall. Upon the urging of whispered voices below, we finally managed to pull ourselves up onto the roof and then immediately scurried behind a rather large chimney. There was no moon so it was a very dark night. It was even colder and much windier on the roof than it had been when we originally started our climb.

Below, as they went door to door, we could hear the Germans barking orders to the tenants. Concerned that I may have left something suspicious laying out in the open, I held my breath as they entered our apartment.

Andre and I did not make a sound. We worried that the Germans might also step out onto the balcony but, as we learned later, Uncle Kees had moved the stepladder.

We were the only ones on the roof. We stayed there about two hours, shivering and huddled closely together next to the chimney, our teeth chattering from time to time.

Then we heard a whispered shout from Uncle Kees, "Jan! Andre! Come, it's all clear."

Although it proved not to be as simple as we thought it would be, we finally managed to climb down off the roof and back into the apartment.

Approximately two weeks later, the doorbell rang, quite unexpectedly. My parents had come to visit me! After a cup of tea, which had been diligently prepared by Aunt Dien, and a brief discussion about how things were going for them and what the future held for us all, they left just about an hour after they had arrived. Before departing, however, my father gave me a 25.00 Dutch guilders bank note and told me to use it in case of an emergency or to tide me over should the need arise. I promised I would be careful with the money and use it only when absolutely necessary. As they walked out the door, I noticed that my father also gave Uncle Kees some money, which I later realized was to pay for keeping me.

During their visit, my parents expressed their sincere appreciation to Uncle Kees and Aunt Dien for all they were doing for me. They explained that they were about twenty-five miles away, in the countryside, where they had rented a room in a large villa with a big garden from a nice, elderly lady. As usual, when they left there were no tearful goodbyes and hugs, just a casual statement, something like: "Well, we'd better be going. Sure hope this war is over soon!"

One day, two other visitors arrived unexpectedly. Since we had no telephone, they couldn't call us. As usual, when the doorbell rang, Andre and I immediately stopped what we were doing and hid in our bedroom, albeit with a small amount of controlled panic. Uncle Kees or Aunt Dien would not open the apartment door until our bedroom door was closed.

On this occasion, the visitors were my Aunt Jetty and Uncle Sam. Uncle Kees had been Uncle Sam's chauffeur before the war. I liked Uncle Sam a lot. He and Aunt Jetty lived close to my grandmother in Utrecht, where we often went on Sundays to visit them from time to time.

When we arrived at Uncle Sam's place, he would always find a way to take me aside so that he could give me a nice piece of sausage to eat. Today, I still love sausage with a passion.

To illustrate why I liked being at Uncle Sam's so much, let me give you an idea how food was doled out in our home before the war. For lunch we would open a can of sardines that would be split amongst four people. Each would get perhaps one and a half sardines. A can of salmon was a great luxury and could last for as long as two days. For my birthday, I might have requested a glass jar of California fruit. Of course, it would last for the usual two days because we all got one piece of fruit from the jar. Then my father would pontificate on and on about how good things were in our house, because when *he* was a kid an orange was divided amongst eight people, if not more.

So, to get a big piece of sausage to chomp on, was a treat never to be forgotten, even by a six-or seven-year-old child.

Yes, they were my precious Uncle Sam and Aunt Jetty, and I just loved going to their house. Once, when Aunt Jetty saw me, she was so relieved, she crushed me to her more than ample bosom, crying over the knowledge that I was alright, safe and in good hands.

On this most recent visit however, it was evening. They said they didn't have a safe place to stay. At the time, they weren't aware that Andre and I were there and thought maybe they could stay for a while. Although Uncle Sam was calm, Aunt Jetty was crying. The matter was discussed and an alternative place was ultimately found to tide them over. Knowing that they could not stay because we were already there, they left but were grateful to Uncle Kees and Aunt Dien for hiding us.

Besides all the raids that were going on around us, we were also faced with a dwindling supply of food in the city. Because Uncle Kees worked as a guard and often pulled night duty guarding some warehouses not far from the apartment,

75

he was usually able to scrounge up some food for us, from one or two of the warehouses he was guarding.

Heating was another problem. The mines in Limburg could not supply enough coal for us because most of it was being shipped to Germany,which left little for the Netherlands. As it started to get cold, we wore warm clothes in the house so that we wouldn't have to turn on the heat, which consisted of a single coal-burning heater in the living room. Since the rest of the apartment was not heated, we soon learned that the small kitchen was a good place to hang out, especially when Aunt Dien was cooking—that is, if she had something to cook. The food supply was rapidly dwindling all over the country. So, with this in mind, my father arranged for me to go and live where my sister was in hiding.

On Aunt Dien's birthday, a man rang the doorbell. He identified himself as Uncle Jos. Uncle Jos was a farmer. He had instructions from my father to pick me up and take me to his farm. Uncle Jos was about six foot tall and solidly built. His hands were large and callused. His face was deeply lined. He spoke little, but he got what had to be done, done. He wore a simple gray cap over his sparse and graying hair. He almost smiled when we met. Shyly, I shook his hand.

Now, I don't have big hands even today, and certainly didn't then as I watched my hand totally disappear in his. "Well," he said," it's about a three-hour walk, so we'd better get started. Otherwise, we'll miss dinner."

I quickly packed the few things I had in a large paper bag, looked at the castle one last time, shook hands with everyone, and thanked Uncle Kees and Aunt Dien quickly. Unfortunately, at that young age I lacked the experience and poise to adequately express how grateful I was as I prepared to leave with Uncle Jos. His appearance had happened so quickly, I did not have time to adequately digest what was actually happening. I had no idea where we were going.

Now, keep in mind that Uncle Jos had just walked about three hours and was now going to walk back with me. His attitude about that was incredibly calm; in fact, it seemed like it wasn't a big deal to him one way or the other. Consider, too, that for many, many months, I had not been able to leave the apartment so, coupled with the fact that I was always hungry for the lack of food, I was understandably not in good physical shape for the long trek to Uncle Jos' farm, which took about four hours. I became tired quickly, because I was not accustomed to such physical exertion.

But Uncle Jos never said an unkind word, even though I knew I was slowing him down. We left the city and after a while found ourselves on a black-gray asphalt road with no footpath. Actually, the road was so narrow, that two cars would have had great difficulty trying to pass each other.

The road was raised above the land to act as a barrier against high water. It also served as a dike surrounding the *polder*. Electric pumps kept the land dry in the *polder* for planting, or so the cattle could graze in the meadows.

The road stretched out flat and endlessly. On occasion, I would ask if we had much further to go and Uncle Jos would patiently respond, "Well, we do have a little bit more to go, but it won't be too far now."

I tried to be tough and hang in there. After what seemed like an eternity, we arrived at the simple farmhouse of Uncle Jos and his wife, my Aunt Beppie.

Uncle Jos and Aunt Beppie were not young people. Aunt Beppie had given birth to twelve, or thirteen, children, not to mention the few miscarriages she also had.

In those days, hugging and kissing were held to a minimum, if there was any at all. As noted earlier, I don't recall my mother giving me a hug, and certainly not my father. Therefore, the fierce hug that I had received from Aunt Jetty when she visited with Uncle Sam at Aunt Dien and Uncle Kees, was difficult to cope with. I was not accustomed to receiving physical affection, or even the slightest signs of love. I was embarrassed and remember that I went limp in her arms, not knowing how to react. When I saw my sister, who was already living with them, there was no hugging or kissing of any kind, just a more or less casual hello.

Aunt Beppie was special in every way. She was such a loving person. When she looked at me, her face would break into a warm smile. And in those days, with all the tension in the air, smiling was not really the order of the day. She did not treat me any differently than anybody else. She carried herself with an aura of sweetness, never had a mean word to say to me, and I would have done anything that she asked.

Although she was not a big woman, she was slightly heavy, primarily because of the multitude of children she had borne. Her face usually had a bit of a glow about it because she used no make-up at all. Her hair, which was salt-and-pepper gray, was always neatly coiled into a bun. Always busy, Aunt Beppie worked as hard on the farm as any man. Churning milk to make butter. Cleaning, cooking, or the multitude of tasks that constantly had to be done for the fifteen people living there at the time.

The main farmhouse consisted of a big room that served as the kitchen, dining room, and living room, all in one. From this room, there was a wooden staircase that led to a trapdoor up into the attic. On the ground floor, to the left of the main room, was another room used primarily to prepare slaughtered animals for consumption, as well as to clean the farm's large milk containers. Off the main room was a smaller room, which was also often used as another dining room. Going through that room led into what could best be described as the parlor/ drawing room, which was only used for special occasions. The bed in that room was used by Aunt Pietje, which was short for Petronella (although Pietje is actually a man's name, meaning little Peter). Unfortunately, I never got to know Aunt Pietje because she passed away shortly after I arrived.

Directly off the parlor was another small room just big enough for a two-person alcove bed—which is a bed that is enclosed on top and three of its side. There were also two small doors that closed off the entire bed area from the rest of the surrounding bedroom space. My sister Ronny and I shared the alcove bed, which was about the size of an enclosed king-size bed. Compared to sleeping with Andre, was like sleeping in a palace.

As for the grounds surrounding the farmhouse, directly out from the main entrance itself was a haystack, open on four sides, with a roof that was adjustable, depending on the amount of hay that was stored there at any given time.

Running parallel to the farmhouse was the main stable where the cattle were kept in the wintertime. Uncle Jos was really more of a vegetable farmer than a cattle farmer. As I recall, he had about eight or ten milk cows. There were also a couple of pens for a few hogs in the main stable, and one horse to pull the family by buggy to the church on Sunday. Goats roamed free. I never understood why, they gave no milk. Maybe Uncle Jos was just an optimist! There were also a few rabbits, which were primarily raised to be slaughtered for food from time to time. There was a shed near the farmhouse that stored the few humble tools that were used around the farm. There were no tractors or heavy farm equipment.

To get to the farmhouse from the main road, one had to cross a small bridge off the dike that spanned an 8' wide canal. That path led past the farmhouse and the tool shed, on up to the cultivated land, past the doghouse where Uncle Jos' watchdog was chained to the left of the main stable.

Certainly, the toilet, which was located outside adjacent to the haystack and basically consisted of a hole in a wooden seat with a large concrete pit directly underneath, was part of the farmhouse, but for obvious hygienic reasons, it could only be accessed from the outside.

At the time, I was still wearing "regular" shoes. Since everyone else wore wooden shoes, this did not sit well with Uncle Jos. However, since there were no wooden shoes in my size, a compromise was ultimately reached when two right shoes were found. And since one was bigger than the other, it became my left shoe.

Now, when I try on new shoes, I always start with the left foot because I know if the left one fits, the right one will fit, too. Later on, of course, a pair of wooden shoes was found that fit me, although one of them was of a different design than the other. But the important thing is that I finally had a left and a right shoe!

I learned that in the wintertime, it was quite a challenge to wear wooden shoes because the snow stuck to the wood. The snow would then build up and in no time, I found myself walking on elevated wooden shoes, which meant I would have to stop and beat the snow off the bottoms. However, walking through the meadows in the wooden shoes seemed to work well because the ground was usually moist and "swampy," and the wooden shoes kept my feet nice and dry.

Oh, how I loved to take long walks through the meadows! But first, I had to walk on the unpaved path that bypassed the potato fields and the field of onions and other assorted vegetables. Since there was no tractor, the land was "plowed" with a shovel, which I was often told to fetch from the tool shed so that I could help turn the land with the others to prepare the soil for a new planting.

I have very soft skin. Even with thirty years or more of sailing boats, I never developed calluses, so that shoveling, plowing the field, was pretty tough on my hands. Blisters developed and the skin hurt, especially when the grains of sand inevitably got on my hands and fingers and acted as sandpaper against my soft skin. But, of course, I managed to survive and tried not to show my hands to anyone for fear they might call me a sissy. After a while, of course, my skin healed and although no calluses formed, it eventually became easier for me to work with a shovel.

Even though I was only about twelve years old, I was proud that I could contribute to my keep. I never really knew how much land Uncle Jos had, but the width of the land he worked was about five hundred feet. As you walked past the vegetable plots, you went through a gate to get into the meadows where the cows were kept. Of course, I wanted to see them milked , so first chance I had, I went with one of Uncle Jos' sons, Anton, to the meadow. Milking was done by hand. Anton was about the size of his dad, but much slimmer. He didn't talk much either, but also didn't seem to mind that I wanted to watch what he was doing.

The cows were waiting to be milked, so we didn't have to go far into the meadow. As Anton sat down on a three-legged, wooden stool and proceeded to milk the cow, I walked around them a bit, just watching what was going on. Well, apparently, the cow was not accustomed to this kind of attention. I was standing to the left of Anton, who was squeezing the teats for the milk, when the cow unexpectedly turned her head, lowered it, and butted me in the chest, sending me sprawling into the mud, missing a pile of cow dung by mere inches. I later learned, that this particular cow was known to have temperamental tendencies, and had done this more than once to more than one innocent onlooker. Laughing, Anton was so amused, he didn't even bother to ask if I was hurt. I, of course, I didn't see what was so funny but you can bet that I kept a good distance from that cow from then on!

I was part of the family now and, as such, was treated as a Catholic.

Every night Aunt Beppie would lead us in prayer. We knelt on our knees on the stone floor, in front of a chair, which was used for support. We said at least six rosaries before we went to bed. At times, there were anywhere from eight to twelve people halfheartedly mumbling along in unison with Aunt Beppie enthusiastically leading the way. And even though she had a pillow for her knees, when we were finished, she would still get up with a moan, although she never really complained.

Although all of this was different and very new to me, I didn't really have a problem reciting these new prayers. I easily went along with it. It was wartime, and I wanted to be respectful. After all, Aunt Beppie and Uncle Jos were protecting me from the Nazis. I didn't give it much thought but, rather, just did as was I asked and what was expected of me. Besides, if doing so made them feel good, I figured, why not?

After going through about three gated meadows where the cows grazed, one arrived at what could best be described as swampland with small waterways that were only accessible by using a small, flat-bottomed boat. And the only access to this area was by foot through the meadows. Only once did I see a boat with two men in it, who had tucked themselves between the long reeds and were barely visible.

One of the meadows had a shed where loose hay was stored as feed for the cows in case there wasn't enough grass for them to eat. The shed was about 8'x8' and perhaps all of 10' high. Since it was located pretty far off the main road, outsiders never knew it was there.

Slatted with wood, in case of a thunderstorm, the shed was also a safe place to hide. The 3" spacing between the slats allowed the wind to whistle through the little structure, which prevented the hay from becoming mildewed.

One of Uncle Jos and Aunt Beppie's sons, Johan, was my buddy. His brother, Gerard, often tagged along with us, but it was mostly Johan and me, which suited me just fine.

One day Johan, who was about my size but two years older and full of mischief, "found" some cigarettes. Since we didn't go to school, if we weren't required to plow the land or tend to other chores, we were free to go just about anywhere we wanted. So, with great anticipation, we went to the little shed to smoke cigarettes!

The brand name was Consi, and there were approximately four of five of them left in the package. We lit up our first cigarette. Well, Consi cigarettes had to have been made from garbage found at the bottom of the tobacco heap. To say that I liked it would be an absolute lie because the cigarette was beyond vile. My throat burned. My eyes watered. I was nauseated. I downright hated the frigging cigarette! Johan, on the other hand, was puffing away as though his life depended upon it. When he asked me what I thought about it, I told him that the cigarette was making me sick to my stomach, and that I saw absolutely no need to smoke a second one!

Closing one eye and crinkling up his face, Johan eyed me through the smoke that had by now filled the little shed, and declared that this was *not* very good tobacco. He thought we should get some tobacco and cigarette paper and roll our own. We agreed that we should find some way to do just that.

A few days later Johan winked at me and said, "Let's go out to the shed. I have tobacco."

Having arrived at the shed, with unskilled fingers we proceeded to roll and light our own cigarettes. Well, if we thought the Consi cigarettes were bad, ours were ten times worse and made me even sicker to my stomach! I told Johan he could keep his cigarettes. I did *not* enjoy smoking and felt that the entire act—something that tasted so bad—made absolutely no sense at all! Although I knew he was acting tough to impress me, he just kept smoking, pretending all the while that he liked it.

Fortunately, later in life, I never acquired a taste for smoking, either. Maybe using the same tobacco I used in the war would deter a lot of people from smoking cigarettes today. I think it would cure even the worst chain smoker.

We were all skinny kids. Johan with his dark blond hair, glasses, and a devil-may-care attitude was very different from Gerard, who had very blond hair and a more serious expression on his face. Cornelius, another son, was a few years older and, again, looked totally different from the rest. As Cornelius was old enough to have to report and be sent to a work camp, he was hiding out from the Germans.

Anton, the oldest son, did a lot of work helping Uncle Jos on the farm. There was a boarder by the name of Chris who worked for his keep while also trying to stay out of the Germans' clutches. Chris, a rather nondescript person, was about twenty-four years of age with dark hair. He smiled a lot and said very little.

Little Beppie, Uncle Jos and Aunt Beppie's daughter, worked around the house like my sister, who by now had learned to blend in like she had been a farm girl all her life. Being buxom, coupled with wearing an apron, she looked like she totally belonged on a farm.

So, at this point, there were ten of us: Aunt Beppie, Uncle Jos, Anton, Cornelius, Johan, Gerard, Chris, Little Beppie, my sister, and me—so many of us, all kept busy most of the time to the point that we seldom had much of it left over to spend time together.

For example, in the morning I usually had to peel the potatoes for the evening meal, and there was always a big tub of them to peel, especially on Saturday when we had to peel them for Sunday as well. On Saturday, I also had to polish everyone's shoes.

On Sundays, since there wasn't enough room in the buggy for everybody, we walked to church—which was about ninety minutes each way. Usually, Johan, Gerard, and I walked together.

The church service on Sunday lasted about three hours. On other occasions, I was dragged off to church during the week so that the clerical brothers, who were serving under the priest, could talk with me. There was one man in particular who always went out of his way to do so. I still remember his smile and many kindnesses. I can't explain it now, but he did everything he could to make me feel "human," for lack of a better word. He was a very kind man, and I have never forgotten his benevolent, good-hearted face. Knowing my background and who I was, he seemed to take great joy in the fact that I would somehow be saved from the Germans. Although now, in later years, I am not particularly religious, I nonetheless tend to feel warmly about the clergy.

One day we received word from the Underground that the Germans were planning a major raid in *Achtienhoven* (translation: eighteen farmhouses), the area where we lived.

We knew that it would be fairly simple for the Germans to close off the traffic on the dikes, so that even a mouse would not be able to get in or out. The landscape was completely flat. You could see over the meadows for miles. Once the Germans had closed the roads and taken position, trying to escape through the meadows would be suicide.

When the news of the expected raids reached us, I knew it was time to go to the little shed in the meadow to hide. So, armed only with a blanket, a bottle of water, and a few sandwiches, I walked out to the meadow. It was November, and it was cold. The wind was blowing, chilling my bones down to the marrow.

In an effort to stay warm, I gathered the straw and hay around me to ward off the chilling winds. After two days, late in the evening, my sister came out with Little Beppie to bring me more water and sandwiches. With the few clothes I had, trying to stay warm was difficult. I can still vividly recall how cold I was.

After spending three lonely days and nights in the little shed, with nothing to do—no reading or radio, not even being able to walk around to stretch my legs, but only to sit and wait—I was finally told that it was safe to return to the farmhouse. It took me at least a day or so to thaw out from this experience. In retrospect now, I wish I had the foresight to put blankets in the shed, too, but then, we really didn't have extra blankets or warm clothes, not even a warm overcoat or raincoat.

It was a sunny day. I had managed to get rid of Johan and Gerard and had gone into the far meadow alone. I heard the sound of a plane overhead, directly above me. As I looked up, I saw a cigar-like object falling out of the plane, slowly turning over and hurtling towards me. It was a bomb!

I immediately realized that there was no chance to outrun it—it was bearing down on me much too quickly. As it came closer and closer, it grew bigger and bigger in size. At that point, I became very calm and said to myself, "Ok, this bomb is going to fall down very close to me. I guess this is going to be the end. Maybe I can survive the explosion if I go flat on the ground with my hands clasped behind my neck and hope it doesn't fall right on top of me."

So, laying down in the grass, I waited for the bomb to hit the ground and explode. I heard a dull thud and tensed, my body waiting for the explosion. But there was only silence. I continued to wait, but nothing happened. Gingerly, I raised myself up, off the wet ground, and looked around to find the bomb. I finally saw it about a hundred yards away from me, in the neighbor's meadow. Hesitantly, I waited, ready to throw myself down on the ground again.

Still nothing happened.

Then I saw the farmer and two other men running excitedly towards the "bomb," which turned out to be a gasoline tank that the pilot had jettisoned from the plane because it was almost empty. Since there was virtually no gasoline available because of the war, the farmer was happy to discover that there was still about a gallon of gas left in the tank.

As the war seemed endless, survival depended on

doing two things: stay out of the hands of the Germans, and find food.

The winter of 1944–45 in Europe was one of the worst in decades, with the lowest temperatures and most snowfall, which stopped the advances of the Allies. They could not move forward. So, both sides—the Germans and the Allies—used this period to strengthen their inventories and positions by just digging in for the winter. Food was getting more and more difficult to find.

On one particularly cold day, a young man knocked on the door of the farmhouse, and Aunt Beppie opened the door.

The young man explained that he had walked about forty-five miles to find food for himself and his family. To stay alive, he said, he had started to eat tulip bulbs, which he demonstrated.

Pulling a pocketknife from the pocket of his trousers, he cleaned a bulb, which was about the size of a small onion. First removing the outer layer, he cut the bulb into small pieces, before popping one of the pieces into his mouth, quickly chewing and swallowing it.

As I watched him, I suddenly realized how desperate the situation was becoming. The realization of war and its horrible consequences was staring me in the face and there was nothing I could do about it. Unfortunately, Aunt Beppie and Uncle Jos had already pretty much given most of their food away to other needy people and now we were all suffering from hunger.

After a while, the young man left and as I watched him walk away, I couldn't help but wonder what was next for him. Would he find something else to eat besides tulip bulbs? I sure hoped so.

So desperate was the situation that one day Uncle Jos decided to slaughter one of the pigs. I had never seen anything like it. Not only the smell but the work that went into it was very new and almost surreal to me. Of course, being the curious kid that I was, I wanted to see everything that went on and was constantly told to be quiet and keep out of the way.

First, the pig was shot with a particular type of gun that had to be held right against the skull, otherwise the bullet would not penetrate its brain. Although I did not help in the process, I watched in wide-eyed wonder from the sidelines as the animal was gutted and dressed for consumption.

Suddenly, we had a lot of meat! Of course, the fact that I was Jewish and was not supposed to eat pork never crossed my mind, as I literally gorged myself on it that night, becoming quite ill shortly thereafter. Retching up everything I had consumed, I felt better afterwards and only then realized that with the little food I had to eat for such a long time, I had to be careful of what and how much I consumed, or I would undoubtedly suffer similar consequences. Anyhow, for a short while, we had food, but, of course, since our supply was limited, it still had to be rationed.

A few days later found me alone, standing in the main room of the farmhouse. Against the wall was a cabinet in which Aunt Beppie stored a rather large ham. All the food was doled out in equal portions when we sat down for dinner. There just wasn't enough food and certainly no "snacks" to nibble on to still our constant hunger pangs.

With the gnawing hunger in my tummy, I moved to the cabinet, opened the double doors and gazed hungrily at the big piece of ham sitting invitingly in the middle of Aunt Beppie's Delft blue plate, a rather large, carving knife laying next to it.

Nobody else was in the room. Because it would deprive the others of food, I was well aware that taking a piece of the ham was absolutely forbidden. This was an opportunity that I could hardly resist. FOOD! Yet, I remember standing in front of this big piece of ham, literally drooling.

Trance like, my hand went slowly up to the knife. All of a sudden a strange prickling feeling developed in the back of my neck. It must have been a sixth sense that hit my nervous system. I tensed up from the feeling that somebody was watching me. I shrugged my shoulders and closed the cabinet's double doors, turning on my heels to leave the room.

Without lifting my head, I glanced up and saw the face of Little Beppie, who was sitting on her knees at the top of the stairs, watching me through the ceiling trapdoor.

Although no one ever said a word to me, I felt certain that Little Beppie told her mother what she had seen. Of course, I had not touched the ham, and while I'm not sure, it seemed that I had just a little bit more food on my plate that night, maybe because I had shown good self-control and not stolen food from the others. But then, had I not known that someone was watching me, would I have taken a piece of that ham? I will always wonder.

Twice a week, I can vividly recall, we got deliveries from the baker, who wheeled around his baked goodies in a three-wheeled, lid-covered cart that measured about 55"x30"x30".

For some reason, we were always his last delivery of the day. The deliveryman parked the cart in front of the tool shed and removed the loaves of bread we were entitled to receive, bringing them inside the house. There was usually no yeast in the dark brown bread and with other integral ingredients also missing, the bread was coarse and would easily break apart.

Because of this, it was Johan who figured out that there were a lot of *crumbs* left at the bottom of the cart. I guess Aunt Beppie knew what we were up to, because she always invited the deliveryman in so she could talk to him for a while. The moment he walked through the door of the farmhouse Johan and I would literally *dive* into the cart, quickly scraping up the crumbs and pieces of bread with our hands and stuffing them into our mouths. We were skinny and young and our entire bodies disappeared into the cart. It was not a lot of food but it helped a little bit, and for a little while at least, it temporarily stilled our hunger.

With the temperature dropping well below zero Celsius, the landscape was icy and the drainage canals were frozen solid. The ground actually creaked from the frost and the continuous expansion of frozen water. At night, the landscape was almost surreal, especially when there was no wind and there were pockets of tufts of mist hovering low above the ground. Sounds seemed to carry farther than usual, like ripples in a pond with no wind to carry, distort, or send them in any one particular direction.

It was still early in the morning when we got up.

RAID!!!

The Germans had unexpectedly decided to raid the same dikes they had raided only six weeks prior, this time because they fully anticipated that they would find everyone in their warm houses rather than out in the fields where I had gone before. Although some of the boys managed to get away into the fields, I didn't, so Aunt Beppie came up with a plan to bluff the Germans.

Everybody got up and was dressed except me because I was "ill," Aunt Beppie would later explain. I was left in the alcove bed, next to which she had placed a small side table covered with a lace doily, medicine bottles, a towel, and a "urine" pot. After all, going out in this freezing weather would be almost suicidal for someone as ill as I was supposed to be.

The stage was set.

Since German soldiers always wore hobnailed boots, it was easy to hear them coming from a distance, so lying in bed that morning, I could hear them coming closer and closer, stopping directly in front of the door of my little bedroom.

I rolled over in bed with my back facing the door and held my breath as Aunt Beppie opened the door and said in German, *"Er ist krank,"* ("He is sick.").

A soldier looked into the room, glancing at the hair on the back of my head. Long moments passed while I pretended to sleep. Keeping my eyes closed tightly, I heard him say, *"Nah lasz mal schlafen,"* ("Eh, let him sleep."). Then he turned and left the room, joining the other German soldiers as they left the house.

Often, and just to be safe, they would casually aim and fire a machinegun into the haystack. Since there was very little hay in the stack, there really was no need for them to do that.

We sighed with relief when the raid was over and counted our blessings that all of the men were gone, hiding in the fields, so that nobody got caught. That night we must have prayed at least twelve rosaries in thanks to the Lord!

Life returned to our usual routine, or at least as usual as it could be under the circumstances: peeling potatoes, polishing shoes, and trying to stay warm.

Because of the cold weather and insufficient supply of food, the latter of which resulted in a severe vitamin deficiency, I developed what was referred to then as winter-hands. Both of my hands would painfully swell up to the point that I could hardly move my fingers. There were also deep cracks in my skin that caused me great discomfort.

Everybody gave advice on what do. For example, I was told that when I went to the bathroom, I should pour the urine over my hands and then wait for at least an hour before I washed it off. Needless to say, everybody avoided me like the black plague most of the time. However, none of their suggestions helped. And since I had no gloves with which to keep my hands warm, I wrapped old rags around them whenever I could.

With the electricity cut off around us, come nightfall, we had to sit in the dark. The Dutch use bicycles for much of their transportation, even today, so to have light in the main room of the farmhouse, where the majority of the cooking was done, we raised a bicycle off the floor. A seat had been attached and a small dynamo was kept turning by pedal power. We would all take turns pedaling the stationary bike so there would be light in the room. It was never very much light, but just enough so we could see each other and perhaps accomplish simple tasks.

The cold spell finally broke, and the beginning of spring slowly started to break through. Although it was still chilly, so far we had at least been able to survive the worst part of the winter. With the frost gone, my hands also healed and I was relieved that I no longer had to pour urine over them in an effort to cure the problem, which meant, too, that I was no longer being avoided!

Although we usually stayed close to the farmhouse, with the weather improving, one day Johan and Gerard suggested we go next door to visit our neighbor, who had a big herd of cows. Of course, a lot of cows invariably translates into a lot of manure.

In order to get the cow dung out of the stables, the farmer had dug a large pit in the soil, which was approximately 5' deep and covered an area of about 60'x100'. Since it was the end of winter and everything was slowly thawing, this area was no exception.

Very cleverly, the farmer had laid several wooden boards over this pit to make it easier to simply walk over the cow dung.

Well, not knowing about the "cow dung pit," I agreed to play tag with Johan and Gerard. When I was chosen to be the first one who had to try and tag one of them, their set-up had begun!

Knowing that I would follow, Johan ran over the wooden boards. Unaware of the impending disaster that was about to befall me, but sensing that I could cut Johan off, I followed him across the pit, completely missing the careful placement of the boards and falling full speed up to my chest in the cow dung. Needless to say, our game of tag came to an immediate end.

Running back to the farmhouse, I was, of course, not permitted to enter the house. I had to remove all of my clothes outside so that I, and my clothes, could be rinsed off completely before they could even be washed. Although it was still bitterly cold, I stood in the open air, huddled by the haystack with a towel wrapped around me, trying to wash all the cow dung off my body. Believe me when I say that it took a *lot* of water to remove the stench! In fact, I had to sleep in the stable for a couple of nights before I was allowed back in the house.

And when Aunt Beppie scolded Johan, he said, "Heck, it was an accident. He walked into it himself. Nobody pushed him." Yeah, right!

The cow dung, of course, was used to fertilize the land. The dung was scooped up into small flat-bottomed barges, which were about 10' long. At each end of the barge was a small, raised platform where one stood, holding a pole, almost similar to a Venetian gondolier, that was used to push the barge through the drainage canal.

I loved being on a boat. Any boat. If it floated, I was happy. On nice, sunny days, and even not so sunny days, I shoved the little barge from one, far end of the drainage canal to the other and back again. With a long stick called a boom, which was long enough to reach the bottom of the muddy, algae-covered water that filled the drainage canal, I walked back and forth on the barge, traveling up and down the canal that separated Uncle Jos' land from that of his neighbor.

While underground, I had heard the story about a man who had a small sailboat that he provisioned and managed to sail from Hoek van Holland to England. This story had sparked my imagination. The thought of being able to take off in your own boat—of being able to escape the Nazis' oppression—fascinated me.

The little barge was like a dream come true and helped me cope with the fear and tension associated with being in hiding. After the war, one of my priorities was to learn how to sail in preparation to be able to have a boat and be able to escape whatever danger cropped up to put my life in jeopardy. This desire, which was *not* an obsession, ultimately led to my passion for sailing, Later in life, through a series of circumstances, I sailed and navigated a sailboat from Newport Beach, California, to Honolulu, Hawaii.

While living in Hawaii, I flew to Curacao in the Dutch West Indies so that I could meet the son of the man who had escaped by sailboat to England. Having found his name in the phone book, I had the pleasure of meeting him face-to-face at my hotel about a half hour following my arrival. I told him how his father had been such an inspiration to me. He laughed loudly, and then said, "Let me tell you the true story."

It seems that his father had a small motorboat, which he tried to get provisioned with enough gasoline to *motor* to England by crossing the North Sea, which is known for being extremely dangerous! Getting wind of his intended efforts, the Germans took possession of the little motorboat, which was barely 14' long and definitely not seaworthy, stopping him cold. He never motored the boat anywhere, not even out of the harbor. As the boat was very small, being stopped by the Germans most likely saved his life, since it was highly unlikely that he could have made it to England in the first place.

I was, of course, disappointed to hear the true story, but on the other hand, it made me feel that after making my own crossing to Hawaii, I would be able to tackle almost anything that came my way, as least as far as sailing was concerned. I also came to realize that my sailing experience gave me a tremendous amount of self-confidence in other areas of my life.

Back to my story…

And so it was, with long boom in hand, that I would travel up and down the small canal that separated Uncle Jos' land from his neighbor's.

As the canal was lower than the land, nobody ever paid attention to me on the little barge. But then, since I was barely 5' tall at the time, I think my head was the only visible evidence that could be seen to indicate that I was even there.

Early one day, without any warning, Aunt Beppie said, "Jos, you or Anton take Jan to the clinic and have him checked for glasses. The boy cannot see so good." Little did I know that the only person who realized I had bad eyesight all these years was my Aunt Beppie!

Uncle Jos took me to a clinic in the city, and I got my first pair of spectacles. For the first time in years, I was able to see much better and couldn't help but wish that I had glasses when I was still able to attend school. On this occasion, the trip to the city was uneventful, primarily because this part of town showed few signs of German occupation.

Springtime came and the news of the war was getting better and better. The disaster following the Allied efforts to land in Arnhem in the fall of 1944 had left everybody deeply saddened and disappointed. The Allied troops had planned to occupy a series of strategic bridges spanning major rivers. Unfortunately, the entire invasion turned into a costly Allied disaster, and they were not able to take out the Germans. Communications, or the lack thereof, seemed to have been the major culprit that caused the failure of this behind-enemy-lines' invasion during which, sadly, thousands of Allied soldiers lost their lives.

While the disaster in Arnhem had slowed down the Allied Forces, the fighting continued. The Allies forged ahead and by spring, news of the war continued to vastly improve. The Allies were even invading Germany and were doing well. We didn't have a short-wave radio and therefore couldn't listen to the BBC. News came to us in snippets over clandestine short-wave radios scattered throughout the countryside.

The Germans in Holland became fearful of the Allied efforts. Knowing that the Allies wanted to liberate the northern part of Holland, in an effort to stave them off, the Germans devised a desperate plan.

At the end of each dike built by the Dutch before the war, undergroundmand partially above ground concrete fortifications had been erected which had, of course, been occupied by the Germans. The forts had various names and were strategically positioned at the end of a dike or where more than one dike intersected. Although I had never been in them, I was aware that many were quite large and that they blended in very well with the landscape, to the point that cows grazed on top of them so that they resembled meadows instead of forts.

On either side of the dikes were drainage canals. As mentioned earlier, sluice gates and pumps kept the land dry so cattle could graze and the land could be cultivated. With the Allied Forces coming closer, this knowledge ultimately led the Germans into making a rather futile and desperate move. They opened the sluice gates and stopped the pumps, inundating the land with water. Within two days, miles and miles of land were under water throughout and surrounding the city of Utrecht. Only the dikes themselves remained above water. The water came even close to the farmhouse.

At the time, Uncle Jos had stored bushels of potatoes in special holding areas underground, which we all worked diligently like beavers to move to dry land. Had we not been able to do so, they would have otherwise rotted and been lost.

We were surrounded by water for weeks. Life became more and more difficult every day. We were landlocked on the dikes and existing high spots above ground. Since this particular area of Holland is very flat, efforts to get to the cows for milking was a major undertaking that almost proved to be impossible on more than one occasion.

Finally, an agreement was struck between the neutral Swedish Red Cross and the Germans.

The pumps went back to work, pumping out the water so the fields could be opened and the Allies could drop food to the starving population. Within a few days after those efforts were begun, the meadows were cleared of water, and I will never forget the sight of the flying fortresses coming so low, you could almost touch them. We could clearly see the pilots and their waving hands. They dropped food at many places. Upon impact, some of the containers burst open, and we grabbed what we could. I was eating dried eggs—just scooping it out of the busted containers—and Swedish bread as well, which was as white as snow. It was so delicious, I felt as though I was eating cake.

For the first time in many years, I had a feeling of well-being from being able to get a tummy full of food at last. People cried with happiness, and I was one of them.

After so many people had died because of lack of food, thousands were suddenly being saved. Today, just thinking about that scene, brings tears to my eyes. There was hope. And I was still alive—maybe somewhat bruised and more than a little unsure of myself and the world around me—but alive and kicking nonetheless and for that I was grateful.

After the food drops, it was only a short time before May 10th that we were totally liberated from the German occupation.

I was standing on the dike in front of the farmhouse when I heard distant cries. They sounded alive and happy. As they came closer and closer, I noticed a man running down the road.

"We're free," he shouted. "We're free! The *Moffen* (Germans) are gone!"

I was beyond joy, knowing that I was finally free to go home without fear of losing my life.

Johan and I went into Utrecht the next day. We were there when the Allied Forces entered the city with heavy tanks, trucks, and cannons. The carnival-like atmosphere was intoxicating and we hollered, screamed, and cried with excitement that we had finally been liberated. It was an unbelievable, unforgettable excitement that I have never again felt since that day.

However, life was still not easy.

The following day, my parents arrived at the farm house. My dad said they had to go into Utrecht and told me to accompany them.

While walking with them in Utrecht through a rather large city square, a man suddenly screamed, "Brouwer! Hey, Brouwer, stop." as he accosted my father.

This is what happened...

My father and mother were visiting this family, a man and his wife. As always, my mother, being the good looking lady that she was, always carried herself in fine fashion. She wore a beautiful pearl necklace, and the wife had commented on how lovely it was. Doing what he had to do, since my father was running out of money in 1944, and they needed it to survive, he smiled at the man's wife and said he would be willing to sell it to them. He pointed out, however, that because it was a very expensive necklace, it would cost them a lot to purchase it. After in tense negotiations, a price of 200.00 Dutch guilders was reached, and my mother removed the necklace, handing it to the pleased new owner, who had it checked out at a local jewelry store some months later.

The pearls had come from my father's retail store. They were made in Majorica, Spain, and had a value of about 15.00 Dutch guilders. It turned out that my father, on this day in Utrecht, had only about 200.00 Dutch guilders in his pocket.

I remember that the husband was big, and he wasfully prepared to beat my father to within an inch of his life. He had the pearl necklace in his hands, which he was shaking as he demanded his money back. My father handed him the last of the money in his pocket and said, "Here you are. I never said they were real pearls."

With that scene vividly etched in my memory, still, to this day, I will not tell a lie because I don't want to have to look over my shoulder for somebody coming up from behind to beat the hell out of me. Yes, my father loved to make up stories—and, yes, sometimes they weren't true. But, bless his heart, he saved me during the war. I do not fault him in any way for what he did. Given the same circumstances, I most likely would have done the same, if not worse. After all, it was a matter of survival.

We returned to the farmhouse.

That same day my parents left for Amsterdam, even though they didn't have a place to stay. As they were leaving, my father said to me, "Get yourself to the store. You'll find me there." Fortunately, as soon as they arrived in Amsterdam, they found helpful people who located an empty apartment for us. I still had the 25.00 guilders my father had given me when I was with Uncle Kees and Aunt Dien.

The next morning I told Aunt Beppie and Uncle Jos that I wanted to return to Amsterdam were I had lived before the war. They, of course, were happy for me. Aunt Beppie made me several sandwiches, and I prepared to leave with my few meager belongings I had packed into a rather nondescript sack. While waving goodbye to everybody, I was trying to figure out how to get back to Amsterdam, about fifty miles away, which I figured would take me a few days to reach on foot. So, without asking for directions, I just started walking.

Here, I would like to mention that after life returned to normal again, we often went back to visit Uncle Jos and Aunt Beppie, as well as Uncle Kees and Aunt Dien. We certainly enjoyed spending time together under much happier circumstances.

While en route to Amsterdam, since I could now move around freely, I really wasn't worried about much of anything. I just thought that by the end of the day I would look for a farmhouse and ask if I could sleep in their haystack. At the age of thirteen, life appeared to be just that simplistic.

I knew I would ultimately reach Amsterdam and

now expected that it would take me about four or five days, walking. I still had some sandwiches with me and hoped to buy some bread along the way.

I had walked at a steady pace for about three or four hours when I decided to take a break and maybe find some water. I laid down in the grass in front of a driveway flanked by impressive steel gates, leading to a magnificent mansion. A uniformed sentry stood in front of the gate, guarding the entrance.

We looked at each other, and I said in my best English, "Good morning. How are you?"

He responded, in friendly fashion, that he was doing well. He seemed to be relieved that I had greeted him in the English language. And I was happy to have done so because it was the first time in a long time that I finally had been able to speak English with another English-speaking individual!

I learned that he was Canadian. In the little bit of English that I knew, I managed to express my thanks to him for being there. I also told him that I was on my way to Amsterdam. When he asked me how I planned to get there, I looked at him with surprise, and said, "Well, I'm going to walk." He looked at my scrawny five foot seven frame, which weighed perhaps all of eighty pounds, and said, "Well, sit down there for a while. I may have a better idea. Just relax."

There was very little traffic on the road. If any at all, it would only be an occasional military truck that passed by.

Sitting on the grass as he had suggested, I noticed the

Canadian sentry suddenly jump out into the road, where he waved down a small, dark blue Volkswagen Beetle, walking over to talk with the driver for a minute or so. He then called out to me: "These two men are going to Amsterdam, and they will take you there. Just tell them where you need to be."

I thanked him and got in the car.

The two Dutchmen were friendly and asked me where I wanted to go in Amsterdam. In less than two hours, I was standing in front of my father's store. I thanked the driver and his passenger profusely, picked up the sack containing my few belongings, and walked into the familiar surroundings.

Although the interior was dimly lit, I could see that everything was in total disarray and that the store was in shambles. In addition to the putrid smell of rotting hay, normally used for packing china, there was dirt and garbage everywhere. When I found my father sitting in his office, I said, "Hi, Dad, I'm here."

He barely looked up and replied, "Good. See those three boxes over there?" I nodded. "Start unpacking them." He ordered. He never asked me about my trip, or how I had managed to get to Amsterdam so quickly.

Here I was, thirteen years old—free and alive—and I had just survived the Second World War.

Chapter Five

Wrapping It Up

Honolulu, Hawaii—2005

After the war, we settled back into a life of reasonable normalcy. I went back to school, although I found it difficult as I had missed so much (four years) of my education. My routine of working at my father's store after school resumed as well. And my mother took her usual place behind the counter to help Dad run the business.

At fourteen, I started to play Hawaiian steel guitar and at fifteen, had put together a five-piece school band. We played for school functions and other get-togethers. At sixteen, I switched to the regular guitar, which I played for many years.

When I was fifteen, I had managed to talk my father into letting me go to a sailing school for one week. I was so proficient after one week of attendance that I could sail a boat in reverse!

When I was nineteen, I went to Australia where I lived for about eight years. After that, I traveled for approximately six months through the Pacific Islands, ultimately arriving in Los Angeles, California, where I found employment in the garment industry.

After almost two years in California, my mother asked me to return to Holland. Following her divorce from my father, she had opened a retail store in Haarlem. She claimed she needed surgery and that she wanted me to take care of the store while she recovered from the operation.

By this time, I had been away for almost ten years, during which time I had held numerous jobs and enjoyed many music gigs. So, by the time I returned to Holland, I had been able to save a bit of money. I stayed in Holland for five years, but I couldn't get accustomed to the old way of living or the attitude of the majority of its people. With the almost continuously gray skies and little to no sunshine, I certainly didn't enjoy the weather, either.

In America, I had my own apartment and enjoyed a way of living that my friends in Holland could never comprehend. At this time in my life, in Holland nothing seemed to be possible, while in America everything was possible.

I married Yvonne, a Dutch girl I promised to take back to America. When we finally made it to the States, our marriage was already on shaky ground. Though we were married for twelve years and have a daughter who is the apple of my eye, I did not hesitate when Yvonne asked for a separation, which in time ended in divorce.

Eventually, I moved to Honolulu, Hawaii. Now, as I reflect on my travels, I understand that I subconsciously moved myself as far away from Holland as I could, because the memories there are simply too unpleasant. I now find myself twelve time zones away from Holland, which is as far as I can go (unless, of course, I were to fly to the moon).

In my early fifties, I started playing electronic keyboards and eventually started writing songs. I recorded over forty-five of my own songs with keyboards that present themselves to me as a gigantic orchestra—maybe not the same as I fantasized when I was nine years old, but now, for me, far better.

My music has brought great fulfilment to my life, and I have published four albums. I don't sail anymore.

My father remained in Holland until his death in 1963. He never remarried. As difficult a man as he was, I still owe him so much and remain grateful that he managed to save my life, as well as those of my mother and sister. Sadly enough, he was unable to save other family members, something that he carried with him in quiet despair to his last day.

My mother remarried while I was in Holland. She died in Israel in 1974.

My sister Ronny, along with her husband, followed me to Australia. She still lives in Sydney. Her husband passed away in 1986.

During the time of writing my story, which has taken almost eight years, I have shed many a tear. It wasn't easy. I'm still living in Honolulu and often have feelings of guilt that I survived the war, when so many others in my family did not. There is this unspeakable sadness that I never got to know so many because they were killed in the prime of their lives.

In 1997, I learned from my cousin Andre about the fate of some of our family members. His son had done some research on the subject and went to Westerbork concentration camp, which is now maintained as a museum. My grandmother, aunt, and cousin were sent to Westerbork. The Germans, with great thoroughness, most likely to impress their superiors, had taken great pains to register every person who came and went through the gates of Westerbork.

Very shortly after their arrival, they were put on transport in cattle railway cars to Auschwitz, where they went from the train directly into the gas chambers like so many thousands of others before them. They never had a chance.

I count my blessings and say thanks everyday to so many wonderful people for saving my life. Hopefully, my music will, in some way, repay all of them for their unselfish efforts on my behalf.

Epilogue

Ronny Rubens

When my father suggested in late 1994 that we take a vacation to Holland, I jumped at the chance. I had not been to Holland for many years and I truly missed the place. I longed for the cold, the image of cows lazily grazing in the massive open green fields, and the algae covering the tops of the canals like a furry blanket.

But our visit was also one of sadness and understanding. My father wanted to impart on me the experiences of the war that were so raw, they continued to keep him an ocean away from the country of his birth.

We visited some of the places that he remembered as a child, but most of the places were no longer there. Things had changed a lot. For Dad, though, I suspect that just being in the general area was enough.

The Creche, the theater across from the zoo that held deportees before they were shipped off to concentration camps, holds earth-shattering memories for my father. It is now a memorial and the surnames of the victims, who were taken from there and killed in concentration camps, are now inscribed on a large black memorial wall. My last name is there in crisp white letters.

A compelling part of our journey was when we walked the steps from the Creche down the street to where my father says his legs gave out while attempting his first escape. We were quiet as we traced the steps of a terrified boy and a soldier.

There, on the street where he met almost certain death, we pulled our coats around our necks while my father told me the story once again.

"Ya, here is vare I fell and da soldier grabbed me by da scruff of da neck." He paused, looking down at the gray cobblestones, "Ya, dat vas a bitch. Dat vas a bitch." I couldn't tell if my father was crying or not. I turned away so that my tears could fall in private.

I can remember the first time that I thought there was something wrong with being Jewish. I was about three or four years old and my mother showed me a necklace that someone had given me. The necklace was a gold chain with a gold Star of David.

As a little girl, I loved jewelry, but I distinctly remember that I did not like that Star of David. I refused to wear it, and my mom didn't push it.

But what I remember even more was the reason I didn't want to wear it. Because I knew it was a Jewish symbol, and I didn't want anyone to know or think that I was Jewish. My instinct told me to veer away from it. I was four years old, and I was afraid to wear that necklace. Embarrassed, even.

Why? Was I already sensitive to a society that looked at Jews as something sinister? Were my Saturday morning cartoons subliminally spreading anti-Semitic propaganda? Or, more likely, was I tuned into my father's internal turmoil. Was it so obvious to me that our secret had to remain so?

For those who survived the war, there was a lot of shame attached to being Jewish. Most survivors understandably wanted to separate themselves from their ordeal. Many, like my father's family, simply stopped all religious observance. They wanted to

119

forget. No one wanted to discuss the catastrophe. If you didn't talk about it, then you didn't have to deal with it. My father spent much of his life burying the secret of his underground past from the people he met. Of course, the reality was that the experiences of the holocaust were still tormenting him.

While volunteering as a consultant for the play *The Diary of Anne Frank*, a costume designer innocently asked my father which Star of David looked more authentic, the one that said Jew or the one that said Jude. Dad hadn't seen a Star of David since he had ripped his off and thrown it in the canal as a child. Seeing one again took his breath away. When the costume designer saw my father in a state of utter shock, she didn't know what to do. They both had to sit down. After recovering, he had to admit that the one that said Jude was more authentic.

That's the kind he wore.

His secret was finally out. It was the beginning of an emotional acceptance for him.

Hearing my father's stories made me a wimpy child and a sensitive adult. Growing up, I knew my father was a victim of the war. He hid his past from everyone except me. I was the lone audience member to his stories. His confiding in me made me feel like a victim as well. I struggled for acceptance under the burden of his secret. I, too, suffered from the terror of being found out.

In part, the reason for this book is to share the burden, for surely we cannot bear it alone, and we cannot keep silent any longer. We must all share our stories and by so doing, we become mindful of humankind's power, good or evil, to command or destroy the world. To listen to the stories of our ancestors is to understand ourselves and to manipulate our future. Who among us would create another holocaust? Who among us would stop it? These were questions no one wanted to answer.

But now we must.

September 11th, was an abominable example of the hatred and insidiousness of terror. Now we, as Americans, know what it is like to wake up in fear. Now we understand the inclination to stay inside. For the first time, our hearts tremble at the thought of the unknown. Now America understands the complete paranoia with which so many others have struggled.

September 11th, brought back the anguish and apprehension of the past for my father. This time, though, he had a daughter to think about. He called, begging me to stay away from tall buildings and insisted that I keep a month's worth of food in my cupboards. I agreed with him. I had already been shopping.

As the survivors of the holocaust get older, so do their children. As Americans, we are all survivors of September 11th.

Most of us don't classify ourselves as survivors, but there is a venerable society of us still forming: Bosnia, Afghanistan, Sudan, Israel, Palestine and Iraq among others. There will be survivors and children of survivors for generations more. Everyone's own personal holocaust will continue. Will we be forever underground?

In the end, we are all like Sallo. We are all, at some point, the little boy hiding underground. And as long as we accept that, as long as we embrace what that means to be vulnerable and scared and a little helpless, then we can overcome it. It is when we forget the stories of Sallo and those like him that we allow the world to become what it is today. A world of hate, intolerance, and violence that would make a man like Hitler proud. A world at war.

Soon after the war, my father began sailing. Something about being free led him to the water, and he fell in love with the ocean and gliding on top of it.

When I was born, my parents stuck me into a life jacket-lined cooler so they could spend the day on the boat. When I was old enough to sit up, they put me in a car seat tied to the mast. My father still insists that was the safest place to be, but I think some people wondered what those crazy foreigners were doing to their baby.

Sailing was my father's escape. It was a complete freedom that he was anxious to keep close at hand. He confided in me that the reason he learned to sail was so that if anything happened again, he could get on his boat and sail away. Escape. That had always been a comfort to him, and to me as well. It's beautiful to imagine that if the world crumbled again, Dad and I could slip away into the ocean and retreat.

In 1978, my father got on his boat and sailed to Hawaii. He didn't sail back. Did he escape like he always wanted to?

In 1987, he sold the boat. When he told me, I cried. I loved that boat and losing her was like losing the greatest playmate of all time.

I like to think that Dad had finally let go of the apprehension of another war, and the idea that he could sail away from danger like you swat away a fly. As if it were that easy.

I suppose there is comfort in the release of that anxiety. Now Dad could move on to other joys, like his music that flourished after he sold the boat.

Yet, I know that his music is also an escape. That he experiences the same freedom in his songs as he did riding the waves like an ocean cowboy.

He told me that the boat had just become too hard to keep up. But I think that for Dad, sailing had always been about getting away and at that point, he was tired of running. He was ready to face whatever land-locked demons he had to. I suspect that in many ways, holding onto the anxiety of using the boat as an escape was exhausting, and that the joy and fear of sailing were inextricability intertwined. Letting go of the boat meant releasing a lifetime of panic and dread. Like a sail lost into the wind, violent and unyielding.

Dad says that he doesn't miss the boat.

I believe him.

Lightning Source UK Ltd.
Milton Keynes UK
UKOW03f1302250117

292849UK00002B/469/P